Teachers' Journeys into International School Teaching in China

Poole's book illuminates the experiences and perspectives of host country national teachers at internationalised schools in China. The international school sector in China has undergone significant changes in recent years. This is due to the growing demand for international education from local middle-class families. In response, a new type of school has emerged. Going by various names, such as private, bilingual, or internationalised, these schools offer a fusion of national and international curricula and are staffed predominantly by host country national teachers.

Despite these changes, we still know little about who host country national teachers are and what draws them to the world of international schooling. Accordingly, this book explores the motivations and mobilities of host country national teachers in China. It identifies three types of teacher: Returners, Reachers, and Remainers. Returners are graduates who have returned to China from overseas study. They are drawn to international schools by the opportunity to use their international experience and qualification. Reachers are internal migrants who face structural inequality and attracted to international schools by the opportunity for social mobility. Remainers are married teachers with children. They are motivated to work in international schools by the perceived stability and security these schools offer.

Discussing implications for teacher recruitment, development, and retention in international schools, this book is an essential read for international educational researchers as well as students researching international education or teacher identity.

Adam Poole is an assistant professor in the Department of Education Policy and Leadership, Faculty of Education and Human Development, The Education University of Hong Kong. His research interests include international schooling, professional learning for language teachers, and the funds of identity approach.

Routledge Series on Schools and Schooling in Asia
Series editor: Kerry J. Kennedy

Supporting Diverse Students in Asian Inclusive Classrooms
From Policies and Theories to Practice
Edited by Ming-Tak Hue and Shahid Karim

Student Self-Assessment as a Process for Learning
Zi Yan

Culturally Responsive Science Pedagogy in Asia
Status and Challenges for Malaysia, Indonesia and Japan
Edited by Lilia Halim, Murni Ramli and Mohd Norawi Ali

The Asia Literacy Dilemma
A Curriculum Perspective
Rebecca Cairns and Michiko Weinmann

Educating Teachers Online in Challenging Times
The Case of Hong Kong
Edited by Kevin Wai Ho Yung and Hui Xuan Xu

Cross-disciplinary STEM Learning for Asian Primary Students
Design, Practices and Outcomes
Edited by Winnie Wing Mui So, Zhi Hong Wan and Tian Luo

Teachers' Journeys into International School Teaching in China
Exploring Motivations and Mobilities
Adam Poole

For the full list of titles in the series, please visit: www.routledge.com/Routledge-Series-on-Schools-and-Schooling-in-Asia/book-series/RSSSA

Teachers' Journeys into International School Teaching in China
Exploring Motivations and Mobilities

Adam Poole

LONDON AND NEW YORK

First published 2024
by Routledge
4 Park Square, Milton Park, Abingdon, Oxon OX14 4RN

and by Routledge
605 Third Avenue, New York, NY 10158

Routledge is an imprint of the Taylor & Francis Group, an informa business

© 2024 Adam Poole

The right of Adam Poole to be identified as author of this work has been asserted in accordance with sections 77 and 78 of the Copyright, Designs and Patents Act 1988.

All rights reserved. No part of this book may be reprinted or reproduced or utilised in any form or by any electronic, mechanical, or other means, now known or hereafter invented, including photocopying and recording, or in any information storage or retrieval system, without permission in writing from the publishers.

Trademark notice: Product or corporate names may be trademarks or registered trademarks, and are used only for identification and explanation without intent to infringe.

British Library Cataloguing-in-Publication Data
A catalogue record for this book is available from the British Library

Library of Congress Cataloging-in-Publication Data
A catalog record for this book has been requested

ISBN: 978-1-032-49972-7 (hbk)
ISBN: 978-1-032-49973-4 (pbk)
ISBN: 978-1-003-39629-1 (ebk)

DOI: 10.4324/9781003396291

Typeset in Galliard
by Apex CoVantage, LLC

Contents

	Series editor's note	*viii*
	Acknowledgements	*x*
	Preface	*xi*
1	Planning: packing key conceptual and methodological tools for the journey ahead	1
2	Departure: travelling through the changing international school landscape in China	21
3	Arrival: considering the motivations and mobilities of Returners, Reachers, and Remainers	45
4	Return: constructing a typology of host country national teachers	77
	Index	*100*

Series editor's note

The so-called Asian century provides opportunities and challenges both for the people of Asia and for the people in the West. The success of many of Asia's young people in schooling has often led educators in the West to try and emulate Asian school practices. Yet these practices are culturally embedded. One of the key issues to be taken on by this series, therefore, is to provide policymakers, both regional and international, as well as academics with insights into these culturally embedded practices and the contexts that construct them.

There is vast diversity as well as disparities within Asia. This is a fundamental issue and for that reason and it will be addressed in this series by making these diversities and disparities the subject of investigation. The 'tiger' economies initially grabbed most of the media attention on Asian development, and more recently China has become the centre of attention. Yet there are also very poor countries in the region and their education systems seem unable to be transformed to meet new challenges. Thus, the whole of Asia will be seen as important for this series in order to address questions relevant not only to developed countries but also to developing countries. In other words, the series will take a 'whole of Asia' approach.

Asia can no longer be considered in isolation. It is as subject to the forces of globalisation, migration, and transnational movements as are other regions of the world. Yet the diversity of cultures, religions, and social practices in Asia means that responses to these forces are not predictable. This series, therefore, is interested to identify the ways tradition and modernity interact to produce distinctive contexts for schools and schooling in an area of the world that impacts across the globe.

Against this background, the current volume deals with an aspect of international schooling in China that has not received a great deal of attention. It portrays through the eyes of local teachers – referred to as 'host country national teachers' (as distinct from expatriate teachers) – the way international schooling is constructed and understood. It provides a lens to view international schools from perspectives that are both national and international. It is a very welcome addition to the *Routledge Series on Schools and Schooling in Asia*,

Kerry J. Kennedy
Series Editor
Routledge Series on Schools and Schooling in Asia

Acknowledgements

This book began as fragments, hastily scrawled in the dark. The journey from scrawl to published book was a long one and would not have been possible were it not for the support of the following individuals.

I would like to begin by thanking Katie Peace and Routledge for their positive reception and support of my work.

Thanks also go to the participants whose contributions made this book what it is. Without their words, this book would have remained an idea gathering dust in the backroom of my mind.

I would also like to thank the following friends and colleagues whose continued support contributed directly and indirectly to the writing of this book: Giovanna Comerio for keeping me on my academic toes and sharing the academic journey with me; Qin Yunyun for helping me to understand Chinese academia and inspiring many interesting academic conversations; Yuan Dayong for giving me a chance and supporting my research; Tristan Bunnell for continuing collaboration and insights into international schooling; and Dave Yan for his unswerving authenticity and reminding me to keep struggling.

I reserve my biggest thanks to my wife, Maggie, and son, Henry, for always being there for me. My wife took care of things so I could sit down and write. This hidden aspect of the writing process is not acknowledged enough. She was also the first person I shared my ideas with and our conversations provided me with invaluable feedback and insights into Chinese education and society. My son, Henry, gave me the inspiration to keep writing. There were days when I wondered if this book would ever be finished, but his passion for all things, Gamera and kaiju, kept me going.

Preface

Between heaven and earth
our lives rush past
like travellers with a long road to go.[1]

This book has emerged from my former experiences as an international school teacher and my current career as an academic in China. Initially, my scholarly focus was on the expatriate teacher experience, emerging in no small part from my own lived experiences as an international school teacher. This expatriate focus was reflected in my doctoral research (Poole, 2019), which examined teachers' constructions of cross-cultural identities, as well my post-doctoral research (e.g. Poole, 2022), which not only continued to focus on the lived experiences of expatriate teachers in non-traditional international schools but also saw the development of an autoethnographic focus. This move towards autoethnography informed much of my first monograph, *International teachers' lived experiences: Examining internationalised schooling in Shanghai* (Poole, 2021). This book encapsulates the early phase of my research, which focused on the expatriate teacher experience, authenticity and voice, and the development of a hybrid positionality. The aim of this early phase was to move beyond the restrictions of teacher typologies and to capture the complexity and messiness of lived experience.

My subsequent move from international school teaching to academia in 2020 saw me continuing to collect data from non-traditional international schools but moving from the expatriate experience to considering the host country teacher experience. This phase also saw a growing interest in approaching international school teachers from a sociological lens of inquiry. This led to the development of two research projects, which form the foundation of this book. Both projects were granted ethical clearance by the author's then institutions (Beijing Foreign Studies University (BFSU) International and BFSU, respectively) and followed BERA's (2018) guidelines for ethical research.

The first project, conducted in early 2021, sought to understand host country national teachers' professional development needs in a non-traditional international school in a rural setting (e.g. three hours' drive from Shanghai). As part of this project, I also conducted a number of interviews with host country national teachers in Beijing and Shanghai, which are also included in this book. While these interviews, which were conducted in both English and Chinese at the discretion of the participant, were primarily focused on understanding teachers' professional development needs, the teachers also talked at length about their reasons and motivations for working in international schools. The teachers' motivations were encapsulated in three metaphors, which form the basis for this book's main empirical contribution. These metaphors are 'Returners' (Chinese returnees who have studied/worked overseas), 'Reachers' (teachers who utilise internationalised schooling for social mobility), and 'Remainers' (teachers who view internationalised schooling in pragmatic terms as a way to realise intergenerational social advantage).

The second research project, conducted in late 2022, sought to understand host country national teachers' perceptions of international schooling in a non-traditional international school in a Tier-2 city in the South of China. Once again, the interviews for this project were conducted in both English and Chinese. The project found that the participants held diverse conceptions of the purpose of international schooling in China for Chinese students and offered evidence of the heterogeneity of the host country national teacher experience. While this aspect of the project is not reported in this book, the teachers' motivations for joining an international school are extensively utilised. The reader is encouraged to consult Poole and Qin (in press) for more on teachers' perceptions of the purpose of international schooling for Chinese students.

These two projects made me realise that my own concerns with authenticity, voice, and lived experience had restricted my gaze and, perhaps, even contributed to the reproduction of an ethnocentric-expatriate gaze. Invoking the pragmatic logic of the bricolage (Kincheloe, 2005), it is necessary to create new wholes from the fragments of what came before. Accordingly, this book eschews conventional sociological tools – such as Bourdieu's capitals – and instead develops a bespoke bricolage of academic and everyday sociological concepts derived from both China and the West.

The journey in the book's title operates on multiple levels. On the most literal level, the book is about understanding host country national teachers' journeys into international schooling. This involves considering their motivations and mobilities. At the same time, the book is also concerned with locating and searching for the host country national teacher in the academic literature, which represents another kind of journey. On another level, the reader is invited to take a journey and explore the participants' experiences and pathways into international school teaching. On yet another level, the book represents my own academic journey, which has seen me move from fixating on the lived experiences of the expatriate school teacher to considering the motivations and mobilities of the host country national teacher.

With the metaphor of the journey in mind, each chapter of this book represents a stage in the overall journey to understand and find the host country national teacher. Chapter 1 ('Planning') considers the terrain that will be explored (international schooling), the key concepts that need to be packed for the journey (motivation and China as method approach in all counts), and finally the itinerary. Chapter 2 ('Departure') provides the reader with contextual information about the international school landscape in China. Chapter 3 ('Arrival') considers the motivations and (im)mobilities of the participants. Chapter 4 ('Return') synthesises the insights from Chapter 3 to construct a typology of host country national teachers working in international schools based on their initial motivation.

Note

1 This is a translated excerpt from an anthology of Chinese poems, often referred to as 'Nineteen Ancient Poems', which were most likely collected during the Han dynasty. I have rearranged the lines so they form a three-lined stanza. The original Chinese is: 人生長存活在天地之間，就好比遠行匆匆的過客.

References

BERA (2018). Ethical guidelines for educational research. *BERA*. www.bera.ac.uk/publication/ethical-guidelines-for-educational-research-2018-online

Kincheloe, J. L. (2005). On to the next level: Continuing the conceptualization of the bricolage. *Qualitative Inquiry*, *11*(3), 323–350.

Poole, A. (2019). How internationalised school teachers construct cross-cultural identities in an internationalised school in Shanghai, China. *Unpublished doctoral thesis: University of Nottingham*.

Poole, A. (2021). *International teachers' lived experiences: Examining internationalised schooling in Shanghai*. Springer Nature.

Poole, A. (2022). More than interchangeable "local" teachers: Host country teachers' journeys into internationalised school teaching in China. *Research in Comparative and International Education*, *17*(3), 424–440.

Poole, A., & Qin, Y. Y. (in press). Nationalising the international in China: A phenomenological perspective on the purpose of international schooling in an era of regulation. *The British Educational Research Journal*.

1 Planning

Packing key conceptual and methodological tools for the journey ahead

Introduction

This chapter is the start of the journey to explore and understand the motivations and lived experiences of Ru, Shu, Jin, Ying, and Gang (pseudonyms), who represent an emerging type of international school teacher in China, best described as the host country national teacher. Host country national teachers live and work in their home country or region and are typically citizens of the country in which their international school operates (Garton, 2000; Tyvand, 2017). As with any journey, it is necessary to plan, pack, and create an itinerary. This chapter does this by introducing the reader to key background and conceptual and methodological information for navigating the rest of the book.

This chapter first considers the changing international school landscape, the rise of non-traditional international schools, and, hand in hand with this change, the emergence of the host country national teacher as a significant yet under-researched actor. This might be thought of as the 'planning stage' of the journey. While some research has been done on host country national teachers (e.g. Poole, 2019), studies on the expatriate teacher remain the norm. There remains a dearth of studies on host country national teachers in China, where the majority of international schools are now the non-traditional type. This chapter then considers teachers' motivations for working in international schools and critically reviews a number of teacher typologies that have been developed on the basis of teachers' motivations. This leads to an exploration of China as method, which informs the book's design, and my positionality as a white, British male academic researching international schooling in China. This might be thought of as the 'packing stage' and involves considering what kinds of conceptual tools will be needed for the journey ahead. Finally, this chapter ends by offering the reader an 'itinerary' of the journey to come.

Planning

Consulting the map

International schooling as a sector has seen continuous and staggering growth in recent years. International School Consultancy (ISC) Research reports, as of May 2023, that the sector boasts of some 13,192 schools, catering for about 6.51 million students, staffed by approximately 626,767 teachers, administrators, and leaders, and worth a staggering 56 billion dollars (ISC, 2023). It is projected that by 2028, the international school sector will encompass about 16,500 schools, educating nearly 10 million children (Bunnell, 2020). This growth can, in part, be attributed to a number of major shifts at the core of the international school sector, which, according to Bunnell (2014), has seen the sector move from an 'Ideal' phase of activity to a post-Ideal one characterised by an increasing focus on profit-making and proprietorship.

The first shift, which is geographical in nature, has seen the 're-positioning of International Schooling' (Bunnell, 2020, p. 2) from the Global North to the Global South (Poole, 2020). Whereas traditionally (during the Ideal phase) the majority of international schools were to be found in countries such as the United Kingdom, the United States, and Europe, in the last 20 years or so this trend has been reversed, with the majority of international schools now opening in the Global South – that is the Middle-East and the Asia-Pacific regions.

The second shift relates to the emergence and proliferation of a new type of international school. The so-called traditional international school (Hayden & Thompson, 2013), which catered for the children of expatriates, has been eclipsed in number by non-traditional international schools, which cater primarily for an affluent and aspirational local middle-class clientele. Significantly, the growth of the international school sector in the Global South has been fuelled by the emergence of non-traditional international schools (Gaskell, 2019).

The final shift, and the focus of this book, relates to shifts in international school demographics. It has been observed that international schools are shifting from an international solution for mobile professionals to a form of education that offers a 'local' base of aspiring, middle-class consumers (Bunnell, 2020) an internationally oriented and internationally validated alternative to national curricula (Yemini et al., 2022). Previously, only about 20 per cent of students in international schools were host country national students (Brummit & Keeling, 2013). However, in recent years, this trend has been reversed, with approximately 80 per cent of students now being host country national students and just 20 per cent being expatriate students (Brummit & Keeling, 2013). Once again, this shift can partly be attributed to the changing landscape, which has seen the Global South emerge as the epicentre of activity.

Mirroring the growth of a local middle-class consumer, non-traditional international schools are increasingly being staffed by host country national teachers like Ru, Shu, Jin, Ying, and Gang. On the surface, it would appear as though these teachers constitute a relatively small part of the overall international school teaching labour force. This is certainly the impression that has been created by recent research, typified by a study (CIS, 2021) carried out by the Council of International Schools (CIS). CIS is a membership community that provides services to international schools that are committed to high-quality international education and provides students with the skills and knowledge to be global citizens. Surveying 175 international schools in 2021 in order to understand school diversity in terms of ethnicity and gender, CIS found that the most represented nationality in international schools were teachers from the United States, the United Kingdom, and Canada, with there being 2.2 more teachers from Western countries than non-Western countries (CIS, 2021). The survey also found that while the majority of teachers (61 per cent) were female, something echoed by Bunnell (2014), only 25 per cent of heads of school were female, suggesting gender bias in the hiring of school leaders.

However, these findings need to be approached with caution, as the survey was distributed to schools that were affiliated to the CIS and other accreditation agencies. The schools surveyed were likely traditional international schools (Hayden & Thompson, 2013), where host country national teachers indeed remain a minority. As noted earlier, the diversification of the international school sector has seen the emergence of non-traditional international schools, which, based on numbers from China, suggests a very different picture. ISC Research, as reported by Gaskell (2019), estimates that the proportion of expatriate teachers employed by non-traditional international schools in China is about 39.5 per cent. This would put host country national teachers in the majority. Therefore, it is possible to assert, although tentatively, that host country national teachers, and not expatriate teachers, now represent the most ubiquitous teachers in non-traditional international schools, at least in China. It has also been suggested that the growing demand for international schooling cannot be met by teachers from the United Kingdom, the United States, and Europe alone (Gaskell, 2019; Venture, 2022), thereby opening up the candidate pool to those residing 'in-country', which would also include host country national teachers. Not only are host country national teachers in a position to carry the burden of demand, but in many ways, they are better suited to the task of educating local middle-class students, as they share the same language and culture.

Overall, it is possible to make the following observations about the international school sector. Non-traditional international schools (largely located in the Global South, catering for host country national students and predominantly staffed by host country national teachers) have now emerged as the dominant type of international schools. Traditional international schools still have a significant presence, but their growth, at least in China, has stagnated in recent years (Chan & Olcott, 2022). Despite growing in number and significance, relatively little research has been oriented towards the study of host

4 *Planning*

country national teachers. While there are some studies on host country national teachers in China (e.g. Kostogriz & Bonar, 2019; Kostogriz et al., 2022; Poole, 2019, 2022b; Tyvand, 2017) and beyond (Brandin, 2021; Hammer, 2021), they do not shed much light on who these teachers are and why they have come to work in the international school sector. This compels greater investigation into their motivations and mobilities.

In contrast, there is a much clearer and vivid picture of the expatriate teacher, who continues to be the focus of scholarly attention by international school scholars (Poole & Bunnell, 2023). For example, Bailey (2015) and Bunnell (2016) called for greater scrutiny of the experiences and theorisation of the international school teacher some seven years ago, but the ensuing scholarly discourse (e.g. Bailey, 2021; Bailey & Cooker, 2019; Bunnell & Poole, 2022; Brady, 2022; Bright, 2022; Hrycak, 2015; Poole, 2021b; Rey et al., 2020; Savva, 2013, 2015; Stroud Stasel, 2021, 2023) has tended to equate the international school teacher with the expatriate teacher, thereby suggesting a bias towards the expatriate teacher experience and/or a lag between theory and changes on the ground. Given the changes highlighted earlier, it is now time to reorient the scholarly discourse from the expatriate teacher to the host country national teacher.

Purpose of the trip

In order to reorient the scholarly discourse, this book primarily draws upon semi-structured interviews with five Chinese host country national teachers (Ru, Shu, Jin, Ying, and Gang), which is supplemented with additional interview and survey findings with 21 teachers collected during the past two years (see the Preface for more). The reader may also wish to consult Poole (2022b) and Poole et al. (2022) for more information about the projects from which these additional data were collected. Although the overall sample consisted of 26 teachers, I focus primarily on just five, as one of my aims in writing this book is to humanise the lived experiences of host country national teachers in China. I draw on Ru, Shu, Jin, Ying, and Gang's interviews, specifically, as they offer the most compelling and diverse narratives of host country national teachers' journeys into international schooling.

China is worthy of scholarly attention for a number of reasons. First, China has and continues to be my main scholarly focus. My previous book (Poole, 2021) explored the experiences of expatriate teachers in Shanghai, but it did not adequately consider the experiences of host country national teachers. On reflection, I realise that I was doing research *in* and *on* China, but it was not necessarily doing research *with* China. This is something I develop later in this chapter when I consider my positionality in relation to the topic of host country national teachers and the need to embrace China as a method approach, which seeks not only to put China at the centre of analysis but also to place China *in* the world. Therefore, I continue to focus on China because I feel that I have yet to do it justice and there remains so much that has yet to be explored. Second, China offers an insight into the phenomenon of non-traditional schooling that has yet to be fully explored. As China continues to be one of fastest growing markets for international schooling aimed at a local middle-class clientele, it offers an emergent perspective on the localisation of international schooling, which might inform research in other global contexts.

Specifically, this book examines the participants' motivations for entering international school teaching, as well as their mobilities. I focus on their motivations for a number of reasons. First, as will be demonstrated a little later in this chapter, host country national teachers' motivations remain both under-researched and under-theorised. In contrast, the motivations of expatriate teachers have been comparatively well documented, although it might still be argued that international school teachers constitute a neglected middling actor in mobilities and international school studies (Bunnell, 2017). Second, understanding teachers' motivations is of importance to school leaders. Given the shift in demographics highlighted at the beginning of this chapter, a new type of teacher is emerging – the host country national teacher. While school leaders may consider host country national teachers' motivations and mobilities to be relatively straightforward, as they may be seen as the same as public school teachers, the insights from this book paint a very different picture. Host country national teachers' prior experiences, qualifications, and mobilities are fundamentally different from those of public school teachers, which necessitate a reimagining of approaches to recruitment, retention, and professional development.

This book argues that host country national teachers in Chinese internationalised schools are more diverse and their journeys into international school teaching are far more complex than have been previously assumed. For example, in their typology of international school teachers, Rey et al. (2020, p. 364) define 'local' teachers (host country national teachers) as having 'simply transitioned to an international school from the public or private sector' and 'being more sedentary' than expatriate colleagues. While this book finds that host country national teachers are less mobile than their expatriate counterparts and will often 'transition' into international schooling from different sectors, there is nothing simple about this process. The verb 'transition' suggests a relatively easy and straightforward process, but the journeys explored in this book are far from smooth or simple. Rather, they are idiosyncratic, disjointed, and precarious in nature. Hence the title of this book – 'teachers' journeys into international schooling'. While many of the participants in this book have not physically travelled that far, either moving internally within China or working in a school 'on the doorstep' in their home town, they nevertheless have had to cover a great deal of symbolic and affective ground, that includes negotiating social barriers, prejudice, and precarity.

6 *Planning*

Packing

Having considered the terrain of international schooling and selected a destination (China) and purpose (to reorient the scholarly discourse from the expatriate teacher to the host country national teacher), I next explore what the academic literature has to say about international school teachers' motivations for working in international schools. This section represents the 'packing' stage of the metaphorical journey and introduces key concepts, which will be used throughout this book (e.g. teacher motivation and China as method) as well as offer more evidence to support the argument that host country national teachers remain a marginalised, yet significant, actors in the international school literature/sector.

Understanding international school teacher motivation

Teacher motivation

Teacher motivation, as a theoretical construct, has gained prominence in recent years as it helps to shed light on who might choose teaching as a future career and remain in the profession (Müller et al., 2009). Although there remains no consensus on the definition of motivation (Han & Yin, 2016), this has not stopped researchers from attempting to offer one. For example, Schunk et al. (2008, p. 4) define motivation as 'the process whereby goal-directed activity is instigated and sustained', while Roussel (2000, p. 5) considers motivation to be 'a process that activates, orients, reinforces and maintains the behaviour of individuals towards the achievement of intended objectives'. In both cases, motivation is ongoing and continuous and is related to an action or end goal. Sinclair (2008, p. 37), meanwhile, defines teacher motivation as something that determines 'what attracts individuals to teaching, how long they remain in their initial teacher education courses and subsequently the teaching profession, and the extent to which they engage with their courses and the teaching profession'.

Researchers have also identified three main types of motivation underpinning the concept of teacher motivation. The first, intrinsic motivation, has been defined as a form of inherent satisfaction in the work of teaching (Ye et al., 2022) and a person's liking of and interest in teaching, both as an activity and as a profession (e.g. an interest in the teaching subject) (Zhang et al., 2019). In these examples, teaching is largely seen as an end in itself. The second type is referred to as altruistic motivation and views teaching as a socially worthwhile job, emphasising teachers' moral roles and responsibilities (Ye et al., 2022). Finally, extrinsic motivation focuses on benefits related to teaching, but which are not inherent in the work itself (Ye et al., 2022). These benefits are often related to money but may also extend beyond these to how teaching is important because of its social influence and status (Zhang et al., 2019). Dörnyei and Ushioda (2011) have also identified social contextual influences (e.g. the impact of external conditions and constraints, such as social class or education); a temporal dimension (e.g. emphasising lifelong commitment); and demotivating factors emanating from negative influences (e.g. poor teacher evaluation or student misbehaviour) as factors that shape teachers' initial and ongoing motivations.

In this book, I primarily consider host country national teachers' initial motivations for working in international schools in China and use the tripartite approach to identity (intrinsic, altruistic, and extrinsic) as a framework for understanding them and constructing a typology of host country national teachers.

International school teacher motivation

Previous studies have identified a range of extrinsic, intrinsic, and altruistic factors that have helped researchers to understand why teachers choose to work in international schools. In terms of extrinsic motivation, benefits and pay (Bright, 2022; Hrycak, 2015; Rey et al., 2020; Soong & Stahl, 2021), status (Soong & Stahl, 2021), location (Chandler, 2010), and class-making trajectories (Soong & Stahl, 2021; Tarc & Mishra Tarc, 2015; Tarc et al., 2019) have been identified as key motivators. Tarc et al. (2019), for example, explored the class-making trajectories of three Canadian families, who were able to use their positions as international school teachers to accumulate and exchange a range of capitals (economic, social, and cultural) and also harness their position as teachers so their children could gain access to an elite international education. Meanwhile, Rey et al. (2020) explored the experiences of younger, Anglo-Saxon teachers and found that while the teachers' initial motivation to work in the international school sector was based on the participation in privileged lifestyle migration and the need to escape indebtedness (i.e. student loans), they effectively became 'locked into a precarious system' (361) that offered little protection.

In terms of intrinsic motivation, previous studies have identified intercultural factors (e.g., Bailey, 2015; Budrow, 2021; Lee et al., 2022; Savva, 2013; Tarc et al., 2019) as particularly salient. For example, the participants in Bailey's study of expatriate teachers in an international school in Malaysia reported that they chose to teach in international schools because they were looking for an adventure to force them out of their 'comfort zones'. Savva's (2013) study of Anglophone (i.e. expatriate) educators based across three international schools in China and the Netherlands similarly highlighted a desire to travel and see the world, as well as the need to be impulsive and make a life change in order to stave off stagnation or frustration with their personal and/or professional circumstances.

Lee et al.'s (2022) comparative study between International Baccalaureate (IB) teachers and non-IB teachers across multiple countries (including China) also found evidence that suggested IB teachers are more intrinsically motivated than their non-IB counterparts as their 'personal utility' was less of a motivation to enter the teaching profession. Personal utility refers to 'the value and/or benefit (e.g. steady career pathway, job security, and stable income) which teachers think they can obtain from joining the teaching profession for their own sake' (Lee et al., 2022, p. 9) and roughly corresponds to the notion of extrinsic motivation used throughout this book. These findings suggest that IB teachers are more intrinsically motivated while non-IB teachers are more extrinsically motivated.

Finally, and to a lesser extent, there is some evidence of teachers being altruistically motivated to work in international schools (e.g. Bailey & Cooker, 2019; Bunnell & Savvides, 2022; Savvides & Bunnell, 2022). For example, Bailey and Cooker (2019) identified a certain type of teacher – Type B teachers – who were motivated to teach in international schools for ideological reasons, based on an imperative to make the world a better place.

Overall, the academic literature paints a vivid picture of international school teachers' motivations, which are diverse and complex in nature. However, as noted earlier, the literature has tended to privilege the expatriate teacher experience, thereby marginalising the experiences of host country national teachers, suggesting 'an under-researched nexus of activity' (Probert, 2022, p. 228). Given the qualitative differences between expatriate and host country national teachers (in terms of their mobility, qualifications, and beliefs), it cannot be assumed that the latter will share the same reasons for working in international schools as the former. While this book offers some evidence of shared motivation (such as benefits and pay), ultimately there are more differences than similarities. As such, the literature on the expatriate teacher may be insufficiently nuanced to capture the complexity of host country national teachers' lived experiences, which include their motivations and mobilities, thereby necessitating the creation of new sociological concepts and constructs that are rooted in lived experiences.

This book contributes to this scholarly construction project by offering a typology of host country national teachers. I have chosen to focus on the development of a typology as it has featured prominently in my previous work (see Poole, 2022a) and also because I consider the creation of a new typology to be useful to both academics and practitioners. I explain how the typology could be used when we arrive at Chapter 4. With the construction of a new typology in mind, I next lay the necessary conceptual foundations for such an endeavour by critically reviewing a number of influential international school teacher typologies. This critical review also supports my argument throughout this chapter that host country national teachers remain a marginalised, yet significant, actor in the international school literature. Of most significance to this book is Bailey and Cooker (2019) and Rey et al.'s (2020) typologies,

Planning 9

both of which primarily draw on interviews with expatriate teachers discussing their initial motivations for working in international schools. I also first briefly consider two older typologies by Garton (2000) and Hardman (2001), as they remain influential and inform the work of Bailey and Cooker (2019) and Rey et al. (2020).

International school teacher typologies and motivation

Garton (2000) initially proposed three categories of teachers based on their contract type. These were 'host-country nationals' (host country national teachers), 'local hire' expatriates (teachers hired within the country and who typically do not receive all benefits), and 'overseas hire' expatriates (teachers hired from outside the country who typically receive full benefits). Significantly, Garton differentiated between expatriate teachers' experiences – albeit in an inevitably simplified manner (Bright, 2022) – but does not extend this nuance to host country national teachers. Partly, this can be explained by the period and context in which Garton was then working. At the turn of the millennium, traditional international schools (Hayden & Thompson, 2013) employing expatriate teachers were still very much the norm, with non-traditional schools and host country national teachers playing a relatively smaller role than they now do. Developing Garton's category of 'overseas hires', Hardman (2001) proposed a typology for recruitment purposes that offered a number of additional subcategories that included childless career professionals/senior career professionals, mavericks/senior mavericks, career professionals with families, and Penelopes/senior Penelopes.

While Garton and Hardman's typologies continue to be influential, they have in recent years been critiqued (e.g. Savva, 2013; Poole, 2022a) for being 'insufficiently nuanced' (Bailey & Cooker, 2019, p. 129) for capturing the complexity of teachers' lived experiences. This critique highlights how the teacher types offered by Hardman assume an essentialist view of motivation and identity that is largely acontextual and atemporal in nature (Poole, 2022a). That is, motivation and identity is seen as something that does not change over time or place. However, identity researchers (e.g. Akkerman & Meijer, 2011; Hermans, 2003) have come to see identity as something that is not fixed but fragmented and situated in nature, changing not just over time but also across space.

In seeking to overcome the limitations of previous typologies, Bailey and Cooker (2019) proposed a tripartite typology based on Hayden and Thompson's (2013) corresponding typology of international schools (e.g. Type A traditional international school; Type B ideological international school; and Type C non-traditional international school). Based on interviews with 20 international school teachers starting an international teaching qualification, Bailey and Cooker (2019) classified teachers according to their initial motivation to teach and their ongoing motivation to remain in the teaching profession. Accordingly, Type A teachers view teaching largely as a means to an end, supporting travel and mobility. This teacher roughly corresponds to Hardman's (2001) Maverick type. Type B teachers view their job in ideological terms as making a difference to students' lives and changing the world in global and ideological ways. Type C teachers are primarily motivated by an attachment to the locale in which the international school is situated and may feel connected to a location because of marriage, children, or personal interest. Bailey and Cooker also offered the construct of the 'Accidental teacher' as a general category encompassing the A, B, and C teacher types. Accidental teachers have not planned to enter the profession but did so as an incidental result of other events along their life path.

Rey et al. (2020) have also offered a tripartite typology based on younger Anglo-Saxon teachers' first engagement (i.e. initial motivation) in the field of international education. The authors identified 'the expat', 'the adventurer', and 'the local' as the three main teacher types that emerged from their research. The 'expat' refers to teachers whose mobility is tied to personal circumstances, such as being a 'trailing spouse'. Their duration of employment will often depend on the partner's contract. Such teachers may not have chosen international school teaching as their first career but are forced to do so due to limited employment opportunities in the host country. As such, they might be described as 'Accidental teachers' (Bailey & Cooker, 2019). Echoing Hardman's (2001) 'Maverick' type, 'adventurer' teachers are younger qualified teachers from Anglo-Saxon countries, usually unaccompanied by spouse or children. Their primary motivation for working in international schools is based on debt alleviation due to student loans. Finally, the 'local' refers to teachers from a domestic background who are usually trained within their country and have 'simply transitioned to an international school from the public or private sector' (Rey et al., 2020, p. 364). The 'local' corresponds to host country national teachers. Rey et al. (2020, p. 364) also consider local teachers to be 'sedentary', often outlasting 'mobile international teachers in the same school, thus increasing stability within an otherwise high turnover teaching environment'.

Both of the typologies explored earlier advance the theorisation of the international school teacher by building on the foundational work of Garton (2000) and Hardman (2001) and offering researchers a number of useful concepts. First, the notions of the 'Accidental teacher' and 'Type C teachers' correspond to the experiences of host country national teachers and highlight how many will transition into international school teaching from alternative careers or choose a school that allows them to remain close to family. Second, the 'local' teacher, despite the poor choice of nomenclature, suggests that host country national teachers are less mobile than their expatriate counterparts, thereby requiring the development of new concepts and nomenclature to understand such differences.

Despite their strengths, the typologies also have a number of limitations. The host country national teacher is either missing from the typologies (in the case of Garton) or treated as a discrete, reified category. For example, Rey et al. (2020) define 'local' teachers as those who have 'simply transitioned to an international school from the public or private sector' (Rey et al., 2020, p. 4). In contrast, expatriate teachers are differentiated according to multiple categories (e.g. the 'adventurer' and the 'expat'). Overall, there is little nuancing of the host country national type, such as the possibility that this category could be subdivided or that host country national teachers might hold multiple and contradictory motivations. I aim to show in this book that there is nothing 'simple' about the motivations and experiences of host country national teachers. Rather, there is a need to complexify their lives and experiences. I might go so far as to argue that the literature is guilty of the under-complexification of the host country national teacher, which has resulted in these teachers becoming a foil for the expatriate teacher, whose experiences and identities are taken to be inherently complex and heterogeneous.

With these critiques in mind, this book nuances the host country national teacher label, as initially proposed by Garton (2000), by developing new labels that are rooted in concepts from both Chinese and Western contexts as well as inductive analysis through qualitative interviewing. These labels are Returners, Reachers, and Remainers and emerged from an earlier paper of mine (Poole, 2022b). In order to develop these terms, I take inspiration from the notion of China as method, which functions as an underlying philosophy and ethic. I next briefly introduce this approach and then explain how it informs the design of this book.

China as method

The China as method approach was initially proposed by the Japanese sinologist, Yūzō Mizoguchi in 1989. Yūzō critiqued the current state of Japanese sinology (the study of China and Chinese culture by Japanese academics), arguing that it offered 'a reading of China without China' (2016, p. 514) – that is, China as a topic of investigation not on its own terms, as such, but rather measured against the world's standards, with the world assuming a Eurocentric perspective (Yūzō, 2016, p. 516). China was akin to a blank canvas onto which Japanese sinologists projected their own concerns, projections, and assumptions. This critique resonates still today, with academics from decolonial (e.g. Chen, 2010; Zhang et al., 2015) and critical intercultural (e.g. Simpson & Dervin, 2019) perspectives arguing that Asia generally and China specifically are still represented as an exotic Other, existing not as part of the world but placed outside of it in a disembodied state as an object of study.

Having made this critique, Yūzō compels sinologists to move beyond an analysis of China that 'renders the country a flat caricature merely serving to reflect the ambitions and insecurities of those analysing it' (Franceschini & Loubere, 2022, p. 5) and to consider it 'as a constitutive element' (Yūzō, 2016, p. 516). Yūzō proposed a pluralistic world in which Europe (or as I call it in this book, the West) is but one of the constitutive elements. However, it is not enough to just be 'intimate' or close to China. According to Yūzō, the goal of a 'free' sinology should be one that 'transcends' China and adopts China as method. That is, there should be a move from what Yūzō (2016) refers to as vertical principals, where certain ontologies and frameworks are taken to be inherently superior to others, to horizontal ones, where difference coexists in a de-centred way. This de-centring and coexistence of differences resonate with the notion of the bricolage (Kincheloe, 2005), an approach that has sought to move researchers beyond the methodological monologism of the paradigm wars and to adopt a more pragmatic (even irreverential) approach that mixes methods, concepts, and academic traditions in a do-it-yourself approach in order to 'get the job done'.

More recently, the China as method approach has been developed and recast in terms of 'China as global method' by Franceschini and Loubere (2022). The need to return to and develop Yūzō's ideas is predicated on the argument that China is routinely positioned as an inherently different and separated Other that is framed in positive, negative, and ambivalent terms. Franceschini and Loubere (2022) argue that China is not just in the world, but it is part of an interconnected world, and many of the things going on in the country or are seen as unique to China are the result of complex dynamics and interlinkages that go beyond Chinese borders and thereby necessitate a hybrid perspective that embraces both 'China in the world and the world in China' (Franceschini & Loubere, 2022, p. 7). China as method has also been defined in terms of focusing on 'China as the center, basing one's research on China, answering questions about China, and putting forward China-based propositions' (Chen et al., 2023, p. 543). I adopt this in spirit, but do not seek to 'tell China's story well' but rather to 'tell Chinese host country national teachers' stories well' by situating my analysis within an interpretative frame centred in China, but one that also dialogues with conventional sociological (Western) tools. Centring China might reinscribe China as exception or China as not part of an interconnected world. China should become the centre, but as Yūzō (2016) implied and Franceschini and Loubere (2022) make explicit, China is very much distinct but part of an interconnected world.

Having offered an overview of the concept of China as method, I next explain how it informs the analysis of host country national teachers' journeys into international school teaching in China.

How China as method informs this book

The China as method approach helps me to de-centre from a Western-centric perspective and to consider the application of academic and everyday concepts from China. This means eschewing conventional sociological tools, such as Bourdieu's now ubiquitous capitals or the notion of habitus, and developing new hybrid tools. China as method thus foregrounds the need to take China on its own terms while ensuring that it is connected to the world. In terms of this book, it means drawing on concepts that have been developed from both inside and outside China. I refer to these as endogenous (i.e. concepts from within China) and exogenous (i.e. concepts from outside China). Such 'bricolaging' de-centres (or perhaps dethrones) the conventional sociological practice of reducing everything to habitus (the habit of habitus) and allows for the coexistence of difference. These concepts will be given fuller consideration when we pull into Chapter 3, but it would be useful to say a few words about them here.

When exploring Returners, I draw on the notion of *rencai* (talent)/*guoji rencai* (global talent) and, the colloquial expression, *haigui* (sea turtle). *Rencai* is often translated as 'talent' while *guoji rencai* is translated as 'international talent'. These terms, as will be explained later in the book, are inextricably linked to China's human capital, economic development, prosperity, and economic growth (MacLachlan & Gong, 2022). *Haigui* literally translates as 'sea turtle' and is used to refer to overseas Chinese who return to China after working or studying abroad. For the analysis of Reachers, I draw on the notion of *hukou* (household registration system) in order to understand how working in an international school becomes a class strategy for social mobility for some Chinese teachers. *Hukou* refers to China's household registration system, which is assigned to individuals at birth, identifies a person as a permanent resident of an area, and determines access to healthcare and educational resources among other things. While social mobility is often understood in terms of class (e.g. middle class/working class), these terms do not map so well onto the Chinese context. Rather than write about middle or working class, some scholars (Wu & Wallace, 2021; Xu & Wu, 2022) view class in terms of *hukou*, which differentiates individuals according to rural and urban residence. Finally, when exploring Remainers, I draw on the notion of the *xiaokang* (moderately prosperous) and *xiaokang* parents (Cutri, 2022), a term that more accurately describes China's middle class than Western notions of class.

Finally, China as method reminds researchers that it is necessary to place China within a global context. China is not just in the world, it is also of the world, and therefore it is necessary to consider the interconnection of local and global forces. In terms of this book, exogenous theories (i.e. those derived from the West and therefore outside of China) still have a part to play in the analysis of host country national teachers in Chinese internationalised schools, even if they no longer constitute the centre. Returning to Returner teachers in Chapter 3, I also draw on Bourdieu's capitals in order to theorise the kinds of skills and attributes that Returners bring with them, which I refer to as 'international capital'. This analysis also entails exploring the notion of precarity, which denotes a situation of structural and existential uncertainty brought about through labour insecurity. Finally, when exploring Remainer teachers, I draw upon the notion of immobility and 'spatial continuity' (Schewel, 2020) in order to understand how staying put can be empowering for some teachers.

Adopting China as method approach also requires researchers to reflect on their positionality. This is particularly the case for researchers such as myself, who might be described as 'outsider within' (Adeagbo, 2021) scholars, who live and work in China but hail from outside of China (in my case, the United Kingdom). As I am a white, Western male researching China and Chinese teachers, it is essential that I explore how my assumptions shape how I approach the topic of host country national teachers. Therefore, I end this chapter by considering my positionality.

Positionality (necessary digression # 1)

At its simplest, positionality describes an individual's world view and the position they adopt about a research task and its social and political contexts (Rowe, 2014). Positionality also concerns ontological, epistemological, ethical, and agential assumptions (Holmes, 2020). Positionality has become significant, particularly for qualitative researchers, as it exerts an often unseen and unexamined force on researchers, shaping the way they look at, approach, and research a topic or group of individuals.

Positionality is both problem and possibility. On the one hand, positionality is seen as something that limits research. It is something that needs to be exposed, overcome, mitigated, and perhaps even eliminated. This tends to be the approach to positionality taken when undertaking doctoral research and has been likened to a descriptive 'shopping list' of immutable characteristics, such as the researcher's identity, ethnicity, gender, and age and how they are dis/similar to their participants (Folkes, 2022, p. 4). However, it is possible to view positionality more positively and more dynamically. For example, the positionality of the researcher could also be appreciated for adding nuance and ambiguity to research, such as reflexivity functioning as a valuable measure that promotes research reliability, credibility, and self-awareness in qualitative research (Adeagbo, 2021). Moreover, as some qualitative researchers are starting to argue (e.g. Adeagbo, 2021; Adu-Ampong & Adams, 2020; Folkes, 2022), positionality is not something that is fixed but is fluid in nature, shifting over the course of the research process.

Taking inspiration from recent reflexive accounts of positionality and qualitative research, I occupy a somewhat confused positionality as an 'outsider-within' (Adeagbo, 2021). I consider myself an outsider, as I do not speak Chinese well enough to integrate, despite having lived and worked in China for many years. I also consider myself an outsider because China still remains a largely homogenous country; therefore, my white skin immediately marks me out as an outsider, albeit one who is simultaneously Othered and privileged by my white skin. At the same time, I am also an insider, as I previously worked as an international school teacher in various international schools in Shanghai alongside host country national teachers from 2010 to

2020. The participants and I, therefore, embody a shared identity as teachers in international schools.

My positionality as an 'insider-within' also shapes the academic terms I use to identify and understand the experiences of host country national teachers in international schools in China. Assigning a label may seem like an innocent enough activity and is frequently treated as such by researchers, but it is necessary to consider the ethico-politics of labelling (Clarke, 2009). Various terms have been used to identity and conceptualise host country national teachers (including this very term). Thus far, I have used the term 'host country national teacher' unproblematically; however, closer analysis of this term exposes assumptions and power differentials that need to be addressed.

The participants did not refer to themselves as 'international school teachers' or even 'host country national teachers'; they simply saw themselves as teachers who worked in international schools. By referring the participants as 'host country national teachers' am I not guilty of imposing my own, Western-centric perspective on their experiences? Ethically, how can I give voice to the participants of this book if I can only do so from a Western-centric perspective? One way of overcoming or reducing this issue is to situate this study and the study of host country national teachers within China as method approach and ensure that the labels that emerge from within the host country teacher category are rooted in China. Suffice to say, the term 'host country national teacher' is far from perfect and is used primarily out of expediency and convenience. As such, I place the term 'host country national teacher' under erasure (sous rature). Certainly, it is a flawed and contested term (arguably as all terms are), but it is the best I have available to me while writing this book. The term 'host country national teacher' should therefore be seen as a starting point from which to develop a more nuanced construct that encompasses the three types of host country teacher explored in this book: Returners, Reachers, and Remainers.

The itinerary

Having considered the terrain of international schooling and packed the necessary contextual and conceptual tools, I end this chapter by offering the reader an itinerary for the journey ahead.

Chapter 2 ('Departure') provides the reader with contextual information about the international school landscape in China. The chapter first offers an overview of the different types of international school in China. As the participants worked in a specific type of international school – what I describe as a Chinese internationalised school – it is necessary to put these schools into context by considering how they are similar and different to other types of international school. The chapter then considers the development of international schooling in China in order to show the reader how host country national teachers as an emerging phenomenon of inquiry have not just emerged from a vacuum but are the product of China's changing relationship with the West, which is seeing a move from 'integration' to a more China-centric position. The chapter ends by offering the reader information about the participants' biographies and teaching contexts.

Chapter 3 ('Arrival') considers the participants' motivations for working in international schools by developing the metaphors of Returners, Reachers, and Remainers. Returners have studied or worked overseas and use international school teaching to compensate for a lack of *guanxi*/social capital. Reachers are internal migrants who are motivated to work in international schools to foster social mobility and overcome structural barriers. Remainers have an attachment to the locale and are motivated to work in an international school due to convenience as well as the educational opportunities it provides for their children.

Chapter 4 ('Return') synthesises the insights from Chapter 3 to construct a typology of host country national teachers working in international schools based on their initial motivation. The chapter also considers the following: how the typology relates to, and extends, existing international school teacher typologies; how the typology might be used by researchers and school leaders; and the significance of the typology for the study of teachers and motivation more generally. The chapter ends by sketching a research agenda for host country national teachers and non-traditional international schooling in China and beyond.

References

Adeagbo, M. J. (2021). An "outsider within": Considering positionality and reflexivity in research on HIV-positive adolescent mothers in South Africa. *Qualitative Research, 21*(2), 181–194.

Adu-Ampong, E. A., & Adams, E. A. (2020). "But you are also Ghanaian, you should know": Negotiating the insider – outsider research positionality in the fieldwork encounter. *Qualitative Inquiry, 26*(6), 583–592.

Akkerman, S. F., & Meijer, P. C. (2011). A dialogical approach to conceptualizing teacher identity. *Teaching and Teacher Education, 27*(2), 308–319.

Bailey, L. (2015). Reskilled and "running ahead": Teachers in an international school talk about their work. *Journal of Research in International Education, 14*(1), 3–15.

Bailey, L. (2021). International school teachers: Precarity during the COVID-19 pandemic. *Journal of Global Mobility: The Home of Expatriate Management Research, 9*(1), 31–43.

Bailey, L., & Cooker, L. (2019). Exploring teacher identity in international schools: Key concepts for research. *Journal of Research in International Education, 18*(2), 125–141.

Brady, B. (2022). "We think you'll make a great fit": Navigating the precarity of being a gay international teacher. *The New Educator*, 1–15.

Brandin, M. (2021). *A qualitative study of host country national teachers' perspectives on belonging at an international school in Peru* [Doctoral dissertation, University of Illinois]. Illinois University Library. http://hdl.handle.net/2142/114055

Bright, D. (2022). Understanding why Western expatriate teachers choose to work in nontraditional international schools in Vietnam. *Teachers and Teaching, 28*(5), 633–647.

Brummitt, N., & Keeling, A. (2013). Charting the growth of international schools. In R. Pearce (Ed.), *International education and schools: Moving beyond the first 40 years* (pp. 25–36). Bloomsbury Academic.

Budrow, J. (2021). Being and becoming internationally minded: Snapshots of novice Canadian teachers in international schools. *Journal of Research in International Education, 20*(3), 211–225.

Bunnell, T. (2014). *The changing landscape of international schooling: Implications for theory and practice.* Routledge.

Bunnell, T. (2016). Teachers in international schools: A global educational "precariat"? *Globalisation, Societies and Education, 14*(4), 543–559.

Bunnell, T. (2017). Teachers in international schools: A neglected "middling actor" in expatriation. *Journal of Global Mobility: The Home of Expatriate Management Research, 5*(2), 194–202.

Bunnell, T. (2020). The continuous growth and development of "international schooling": The notion of a "transitionary phase". *Compare: A Journal of Comparative and International Education, 50*(5), 764–768.

Bunnell, T., & Poole, A. (2022). (Re) Considering "precarious privilege" within international schooling: Expatriate teachers' perceptions in China of being marginalised and undervalued. *Educational Studies*, 1–15.

Bunnell, T., & Savvides, N. (2022). The united world college experience and its framing: The evidence from a residential short course. *International Studies in Sociology of Education*, 1–19.

Chan, H., & Olcott, E. (2022). China's international school sector threatened by COVID and crackdown. *Financial Times.* www.ft.com/content/2ae60e40-2c95-47ad-9c97-47ef643fad80

Chandler, J. (2010). The role of location in the recruitment and retention of teachers in international schools. *Journal of Research in International Education, 9*(3), 214–226.

Chen, K. H. (2010). *Asia as method: Toward deimperialization.* Duke University Press.

Chen, Y., Lu, A. J., & Wu, A. X. (2023). "China" as a "black box?" Rethinking methods through a sociotechnical perspective. *Information, Communication & Society*, 1–17.

CIS. (2021). Determining the diversity baseline in international schools. *CIS.* www.cois.org/about-cis/news/post/~board/perspectives-blog/post/what-the-data-tells-us-about-diversity-in-international-school-teaching-staff-and-leadership

Clarke, M. (2009). The ethico-politics of teacher identity. *Educational Philosophy and Theory, 41*(2), 185–200.

Cutri, J. E. (2022). *The localisation of Australian elite education within China: A case-study of various social actors' experiences at a Sino-Australian senior school.* Monash University. Doctoral. Thesis. https://doi.org/10.26180/21323604.v1

Dörnyei, Z., & Ushioda, E. (2011). *Teaching and researching: Motivation* (2nd ed.). Longman Pearson.

Folkes, L. (2022). Moving beyond "shopping list" positionality: Using kitchen table reflexivity and in/visible tools to develop reflexive qualitative research. *Qualitative Research,* 14687941221098922.

Franceschini, I., & Loubere, N. (2022). *Global China as method*. Cambridge University Press.

Garton, B. (2000). Recruitment of teachers for international education. In M. Hayden & J. J. Thompson (Eds.), *International schools and international education: Improving teaching, management and quality* (pp. 145–157). Kogan.

Gaskell, R. (2019). The growing popularity of international K-12 schools in China. *ICF Monitor*. https://monitor.icef.com/2019/04/growing-popularity-of-international-k-12-schools-in-china/growing-popularity-of-international-k-12-schools-in-china-2/

Hammer, L. L. (2021). *Exploring the ethnic gap in teacher salaries in international schools* [Doctoral thesis, Wilkes University]. Proquest. www.proquest.com/openview/870eda82d9e626ed0bd31833924eaa53/1?pq-origsite=gscholar&cbl=18750&diss=y

Han, J., & Yin, H. (2016). Teacher motivation: Definition, research development and implications for teachers. *Cogent Education, 3*(1), 1217819.

Hardman, J. (2001). Improving recruitment and retention of quality overseas teacher. In S. Blandford & M. Shaw (Eds.), *Managing international schools* (pp. 123–135). Routledge Falmer.

Hayden, M., & Thompson, J. (2013). International schools: Antecedents, current issues and metaphors for the future. In R. Pearce (Ed.), *International education and schools: Moving beyond the first 40 years* (pp. 3–24). Bloomsbury Academic.

Hermans, H. J. (2003). The construction and reconstruction of a dialogical self. *Journal of Constructivist Psychology, 16*(2), 89–130.

Holmes, A. G. D. (2020). Researcher positionality – A consideration of its influence and place inqualitative research – A new researcher guide. *Shanlax International Journal of Education, 8*(4), 1–10.

Hrycak, J. (2015). Home and away: An inquiry into home-based and overseas teacher perceptions regarding international schools. *Journal of Research in International Education, 14*(1), 29–43.

ISC. (2023). *ISC research*. https://iscresearch.com

Kincheloe, J. (2005). On to the next level: Continuing the conceptualization of the bricolage. *Qualitative Inquiry, 11*(3), 323–350.

Kostogriz, A., Adams, M., & Bonar, G. (2022). Affective practice architectures of professional learning in international schools. *Studies in Continuing Education, 44*(2), 247–265.

Kostogriz, A., & Bonar, G. (2019). The relational work of international teachers: A case study of a Sino-Foreign school. *Transitions: Journal of Transient Migration, 3*(2), 127–144.

Lee, M., Mo, Y., Wright, E., Lin, W., Kim, J. W., Bellibas, M., Faigen, B., Gumus, S., Ryoo, J. H., & Tarc, P. (2022). *Decoding the IB teacher professional: A comparative study of Australia, Canada, China, Denmark, South Korea, Taiwan, Turkey, and the United States*. International Baccalaureate Organization.

MacLachlan, I., & Gong, Y. (2022). China's new age floating population: Talent workers and drifting elders. *Cities, 131*, 103960.

Müller, K., Alliata, R., & Benninghoff, F. (2009). Attracting and retaining teachers: A question of motivation. *Educational Management Administration and Leadership, 37*(5), 574–599.

Poole, A. (2019). I am an internationalising teacher: A Chinese English teacher's experiences of becoming an international teacher. *International Journal of Comparative Education and Development, 21*(1), 31–45.

Poole, A. (2020). Decoupling Chinese internationalised schools from normative constructions of the international school. *Compare: A Journal of Comparative and International Education, 50*(3), 447–454.

Poole, A. (2021a). From recalcitrance to rapprochement: Tinkering with a working-class academic bricolage of "critical empathy". *Discourse: Studies in the Cultural Politics of Education*, 1–13.

Poole, A. (2021b). *International teachers' lived experiences: Examining internationalised schooling in Shanghai*. Springer Nature.

Poole, A. (2022a). Beyond the tyranny of the typology: Moving from labelling to negotiating international school teachers' identities. *Educational Review*, 1–15.

Poole, A. (2022b). More than interchangeable "local" teachers: Host country teachers' journeys into internationalised school teaching in China. *Research in Comparative and International Education*, 17454999221078390.

Poole, A., & Bunnell, T. (2023). A literature review of teachers in "international schools": An emerging field of inquiry. *Compare: A Journal of Comparative and International Education*. https://doi.org/10.1080/03057925.2023.2212110

Poole, A., Liujinya, Y., & Yue, S. (2022). "We're away from everything": Understanding the struggles faced by internationalized schools in non-urban contexts in China. *Sage Open, 12*(1), 21582440221081026.

Probert, S. (2022). China: The under-researched nexus of activity. *Journal of Research in International Education, 21*(3), 228–241.

Rey, J., Bolay, M., & Gez, Y. N. (2020). Precarious privilege: Personal debt, lifestyle aspirations and mobility among international school teachers. *Globalisation, Societies and Education, 18*(4), 361–373.

Roussel, P. (2000). La motivation au travail – Concept et theories. *Notes du Laboratoire Interdisciplinaire de Recherché Sur Les Ressources Humaines et l'Emploi (LIRHE)*. LIRHE.

Rowe, W. E. (2014). Positionality. In D. Coghlan & M. Brydon-Miller (Eds.), *The Sage encyclopedia of action research* (pp. 627–628). Sage.

Savva, M. (2013). International schools as gateways to the intercultural development of North-American teachers. *Journal of Research in International Education, 12*(3), 214–227.

Savva, M. (2015). Characteristics of the international educator and the strategic role of critical incidents. *Journal of Research in International Education, 14*(1), 16–28.

Savvides, N., & Bunnell, T. (2022). The United World College movement in practice: The role of interaction rituals in releasing positive emotional energy to "spark change". *Compare: A Journal of Comparative and International Education*, 1–18.

Schewel, K. (2020). Understanding immobility: Moving beyond the mobility bias in migration studies. *International Migration Review, 54*(2), 328–355.

Schunk, D. H., Pintrich, P. R., & Meece, J. L. (2008). *Motivation in education: Theory, research, and application*. Pearson.

Simpson, A., & Dervin, F. (2019). Global and intercultural competences for whom? By whom? For what purpose?: An example from the Asia Society and the OECD. *Compare: A Journal of Comparative and International Education, 49*(4), 672–677.

Sinclair, C. (2008). Initial and changing student teacher motivation and commitment to teaching. *Asia-Pacific Journal of Teacher Education, 36*, 79–104. http://doi.org/10.1080/13598660801971658

Soong, H., & Stahl, G. (2021). Negotiating "global middle-class" teacher professionalism: Using transnational habitus to explore the experiences of teacher expatriates in Shanghai. *International Journal of Qualitative Studies in Education*, 1–14.

Stroud Stasel, R. (2021). Towards an acculturation framework for K-12 educators who live and work abroad: The role of teacher training institutions. *Journal of Higher Education Policy and Leadership Studies*, *2*(4), 53–75.

Stroud Stasel, R. (2023). Sojourning educators at international schools overseas and the COVID-19 Pandemic. *The Canadian Journal of Action Research*, *23*(2), 107–129.

Tarc, P., & Mishra Tarc, A. (2015). Elite international schools in the Global South: Transnational space, class relationalities and the "middling" international schoolteacher. *British Journal of Sociology of Education*, *36*(1), 34–52.

Tarc, P., Mishra Tarc, A., & Wu, X. (2019). Anglo-Western international school teachers as global middle class: Portraits of three families. *Discourse: Studies in the Cultural Politics of Education*, *40*(5), 666–681.

Tyvand, R. (2017). *Split labor markets in international schools: Perceptions of fairness among local-hire teachers* [Doctoral thesis, George Fox University]. Digital Commons. https://digitalcommons.georgefox.edu/cgi/viewcontent.cgi?article=1100&=&context=edd&=&seiredir=1&referer=https%253A%252F%252Fscholar.google.com%252Fscholar%253Fhl%253Den%2526as_sdt%253D0%25252C5%2526q%253DTyvand%25252C%252B2017%252Binternational%252Bschools%252Bchina%2526btnG%253D#search=%22Tyvand%2C%202017%20international%20schools%20china%22

Venture. (2022). So you want to teach? Teacher development in China November 2022. *Venture*. www.ventureeducation.org/_files/ugd/f23541_14f2f1db450c492eaeb20dfcaa020875.pdf

Wu, Q., & Wallace, M. (2021). *Hukou* stratification, class structure, and earnings in transitional China. *Chinese Sociological Review*, *53*(3), 223–253.

Xu, D., & Wu, X. (2022). Separate and unequal: *Hukou*, school segregation, and educational inequality in urban China. *Chinese Sociological Review*, *54*(5), 433–457.

Ye, W., Ding, Y., Han, X., & Ye, W. (2022). Pre-service teachers' teaching motivation and perceptions of teacher morality in China. *Educational studies*, 1–18.

Yemini, M., Lee, M., & Wright, E. (2022). Straddling the global and national: The emerging roles of international schooling. *Educational Review*, *74*(1), 1–5.

Yūzō, M. (2016). China as method. *Inter-Asia Cultural Studies*, *17*(4), 513–518.

Zhang, H., Chan, P. W. K., & Kenway, J. (2015). *Asia as method in education studies*. Routledge.

Zhang, L., Yu, S., & Liu, H. (2019). Understanding teachers' motivation for and commitment to teaching: Profiles of Chinese early career, early childhood teachers. *Teachers and Teaching*, *25*(7), 890–914.

2 Departure

Travelling through the changing international school landscape in China

Introduction

This chapter represents the second stage of the journey to understand host country national teachers' motivations and mobilities and involves travelling through the changing international school landscape in China. Along the way, we make a number of disembarkations, which can be thought of as contexts for understanding the experiences and motivations of host country national teachers. Out first disembarkation involves taking a lighting tour of the different types of international school in China. As the participants worked in a specific type of international school – what I describe as a Chinese internationalised school – it is necessary to put these schools into context by considering how they compare to other types of international schools. Doing so also helps to clarify why host country national teachers, in China at least, are more likely to be found in Chinese internationalised schools rather than traditional international schools, which continue to favour hiring expatriate teachers from the Anglophone North, such as the United Kingdom and the United States (Bunnell & Atkinson, 2020).

The second disembarkation involves taking a trip through time in order to explore the development of international schooling in China over the past 40 years or so. This will show how the emergence of host country national teachers is the product of China's changing relationship with the West, which is seeing a move from 'integration' to a more China-centric position, as well as increased return migration of overseas Chinese talents.

The third disembarkation will see us pulling into our destination (the participants' teaching contexts) and finally meeting the participants themselves (Ru, Shu, Jin, Ying, and Gang), who will briefly introduce their previous working and educational experiences. This contextual information will become significant in Chapter 3 when the participants' journeys into international schooling are explored in more depth.

Disembarkation # 1: Types of international school in China

Over the past decade, the number of accredited international schools in China has increased rapidly, with the industry (as of 2021) being reportedly worth 46.2 billion yuan (or just over 5 billion pounds) (Ma, 2023). International schools in China should not be seen as a homogeneous group (Ma, 2023) but represent a loose assemblage of schools that offer some form of international curriculum to Chinese host country national students. Three main types of school constitute this assemblage: International programmes within mainstream public school systems; Schools for Children of Foreign Personnel (SCFPs); and private internationalised schools (sometimes referred to as *minban* or private bilingual schools).

International programmes within mainstream public schools

International divisions usually exist as special departments that contain their own teaching staff, international curriculum, and independent classrooms and dormitories. In addition, international divisions coexist with general classes, which teach national curricula, hire international faculty, provide both national compulsory courses and international curricula, and aim to cultivate domestic and foreign students with academic and intercultural abilities (Qian, 2019; Tang, 2014). In 2019, there were approximately 218 international high school divisions, representing approximately 33 per cent of the international school market (Qian, 2019). Examples of international divisions include: Shanghai High School International Division, High School Affiliated to Renmin University of China Joint Program, and Beijing No.4 High School International Class. However, some Chinese scholars (e.g. Sun, 2014; Tang, 2004) regard schools such as Shanghai High School International Division as a distinct type of international school, rather than a supplementary institution, as the school has international teaching staff, an international student body, an international curriculum, and cross-cultural communication (Qian, 2019). Given that these schools are not owned by foreigners or have foreigners sitting on their board of governors, they would seem to fit somewhere between SCFPs and private internationalised schools, once again highlighting the heterogeneity of the international school market in China.

Schools for Children of Foreign Personnel

SCFPs cater to China's expatriate population. Unlike other Asia-Pacific countries (such as Japan, Thailand, Malaysia, and Vietnam), the Chinese government currently does not allow Chinese nationals to attend SCFPs (Wu & Koh, 2022a). However, many Chinese families circumvent this restriction by acquiring an overseas passport for their child/children. Moreover, as will be explored next, alternative pathways into international schooling and overseas higher education have emerged for middle-class Chinese families in the form of private internationalised schools, which serve a similar function as 'channels of global mobility for higher education' (Wright & Mulvey, 2022, p. 2). SCFP schools are comparable to traditional international schools (Hayden & Thompson, 2013). SCFPs could also be seen as examples of 'elite international schools' (Bunnell, 2022; Lee & Wright, 2016; Tarc & Mishra Tarc, 2015), which have been defined as 'a body of well-established K-12 schools teaching the globally mobile expatriate community in English largely outside an English-speaking nation' (Bunnell, 2022, p. 1) and are 'notable for their global orientation in terms of student and staff, curricula offered (i.e. the International Baccalaureate Diploma Programme (IBDP)), and the destinations of graduates for university studies' (Lee & Wright, 2016, p. 121). Examples of these schools in China include Shanghai American School and International School of Beijing.

Private internationalised schools

Private internationalised schools (henceforth referred to as 'internationalised schools') cater for affluent Chinese families aspiring for international education that transits to (higher) education overseas and broadly correspond to Hayden and Thompson's (2013) non-traditional school. These schools remain loosely defined and encompass various private schools that adopt international curriculum elements using English or bilingual medium of instruction (Wu & Koh, 2022a). While these schools offer K–12 education, this book focuses on teachers in high schools (Grades 10 to 12), as this is the period during which students will officially start studying an international curriculum. Figure 2.1 presents an overview of the number of international schools in China through 2019. Collectively, private internationalised schools account for the majority of international schools across China, compared with only about 15 per cent of 'traditional' international schools (Qian, 2019). It can be seen that private internationalised schools are not only the most numerous, but they have also seen the most growth in recent years. SCFPs, in contrast, have all but stagnated, perhaps due to the impact of the global pandemic and growing geopolitical tensions between China and the United States.

Typically, internationalised schools offer some form of international curriculum, such as Cambridge's International General Certificate of Secondary Education (IGCSE) (Grade 10) and A Level (Grades 11 and 12) or the IBDP (Grades 11 and 12). Students are only able to study an international curriculum after Grade 9; prior to this, they must follow the Chinese national curriculum. Internationalised schools had emerged due to favourable government policies and a growing Chinese middle class who were able to exercise school choice (Poole, 2020). However, as will be discussed later, the international school landscape has now pivoted from policies that facilitate rapid expansion to policies that regulate international schooling for Chinese citizens in order

24 Departure

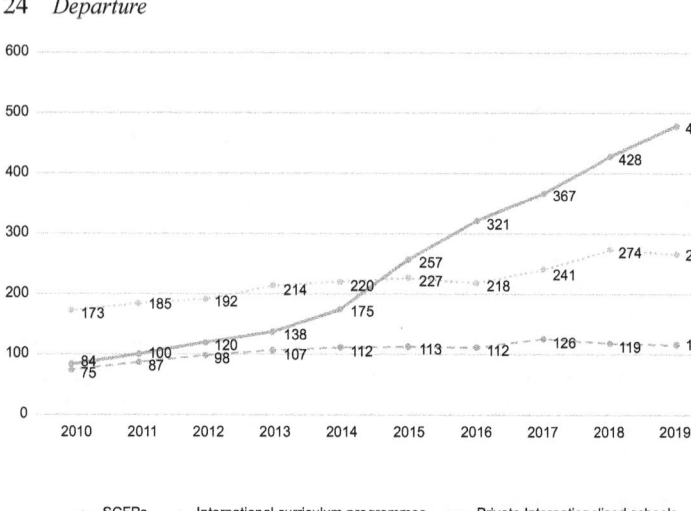

Figure 2.1 Number of international schools in China from 2010 to 2019.
Source: Adapted from Wu (2022).

to avoid 'rampant expansion and retain influence, which is tied to efforts to cultivate national identities' (Wright, Ma et al., 2022, p. 238).

Internationalised schools are part of the local education system and compete with prestigious public schools for students from elite families (Kim & Mobrand, 2019). These elite families frequently perceive internationalised schools as offering a superior form of education to that offered by the public education system, which, despite reform, remains examination-focused and thereby places a great deal of pressure on children who must compete for limited spaces at China's top universities (Cao, 2021). An international education is considered to be superior not necessarily because of its academic rigour but arguably because it fosters international-mindedness and functions as a passport to an overseas university, both of which are considered to be valuable forms of 'cosmopolitan' and 'international' capital (these will be discussed in Chapter 3).

Research by Young (2018) shows that internationalised schools can function as 'refuge schools' (Delval, 2022) for precariously privileged students who are unable to access the most academically selective institutions (e.g. leading universities, such as Tsinghua or Peking) due to poor examination scores in the high-stakes university entrance examination (the Gao Kao) and/or discrimination. These students are precariously privileged because though their parents have economic resources and are part of China's middle class they nevertheless hold precarious social positions as internal migrants or members of China's 'new rich' entrepreneurial class (Young, 2018). Due to the parents' precarious position, they often lack key symbolic resources (e.g. cosmopolitan capital, social capital, and cultural capital) to pass on newly acquired advantages to their children. Significantly, sending their child(ren) to an international school and then on to an overseas university becomes a form of 'outsourced' concerted cultivation (Ma & Wright, 2021) that not only offers children a second chance but also becomes a class-making consolidation activity designed to create those symbolic resources that will facilitate the move from precarity to stability.

Although internationalised school have been described as 'a good with special value for Chinese middle Class' (Cao, 2021, p. 963) – for example, they are used as a utility tool by the middle class to secure status and education resources for their children (Cao, 2021) – they are nonetheless elitist in nature. Although the tuition fees of private schools are lower than those of SCFPs, the fees are still relatively high. According to Smart Shanghai (2021), internationalised schools can charge about 129,600 RMB (about 15,000 British pounds) for Early Years, 76,000–156,000 RMB (about 9,000–18,000 British Pounds) for primary school, and 76,000–230,000 RMB (about 9,000–26,000 British pounds) for High School. Clearly, such prices are affordable only for the upper echelons of China's middle class, who constitute a privileged elite. Therefore, from a critical sociological perspective, private international schools allow parents to secure advantage for their children (Wright, Ma et al., 2022), thereby facilitating the perpetuation of social inequality on a national, and perhaps even global, scale (Poole, 2017).

Synthesising recent research (e.g. Alexander, 2023; Cutri, 2022; Poole, 2021; Poole et al., 2022; Wright, Ma et al., 2022; Wu & Koh, 2022a, 2022b; Wu & Tarc, 2021), it is possible to offer a typology of private internationalised schools in China. This typology is inspired by Wu and Koh's (2022a) typology that identifies schools based on the country origins of the international curricula adopted by the school.

American style (meishi)

American-style (*meishi*) schools are diverse in nature and, according to Wu and Koh (2022a), may only have a tenuous connection to the United States, thereby making it challenging to identify a shared conception of what an American-style international education may entail for Chinese students. Despite this, these schools can be differentiated by their curriculum. Some schools integrate the Chinese national curriculum with preparatory courses for American standardised examinations needed for US college applications. Other schools import academic programmes developed by US-based education organisations (Wu & Koh, 2022a). There are also differences in terms of ownership and management. Although most *meishi* schools are for-profit and private, some take semi-public forms and may be affiliated to Chinese public high schools as their fee-paying international departments (Wu & Koh, 2022a). According to Education Destination Asia (EDA) (2023), there are 46 American curriculum schools in China, although this number also includes SCFPs.

Sino-Canadian style (zhongjia)

Canadian-style international schools in China are known as 'Canadian offshore schools' in Canada's educational policy. Such schools function in various forms, but all operate as private autonomous divisions of larger Chinese schools (Wu & Koh, 2022a). Most are established as joint programmes between Chinese high schools and the Canadian provincial ministries of education (Alexander, 2023). Certified teachers from Canada teach the Canadian curriculum according to provincial learning standards. Upon the fulfilment of academic requirements and assessments, students usually receive a Canadian certificate of graduation issued in addition to a Chinese high school diploma. As of 2022, there were approximately 22 Sino-Canadian schools in operation (Alexander, 2023). Examples of Sino-Canadian schools include Beijing Concord College of Sino-Canada and Canadian Trillium College (Shanghai). It is also important to note that Canadian offshore schools are sometimes not considered international schools, as they are perceived by some as being distinct in terms of the student composition (serving citizens of the local society rather than expatriate communities), ownership (proprietary and for-profit), and curriculum delivery (Canadian curriculum, but with some mandatory subjects in Mandarin by Chinese teachers) (Wang, 2017). However, the demand from local middle-class Chinese parents has led to the blurring of the line between offshore and international schools (Wang, 2017).

British style (yingshi)

International British-style (*yingshi*) schools fall into two categories. The first type adopts international curricula with a UK origin, typically the British A Level and the IGCSE. Usually, this type of school is established in China and operates under local brands (Wu & Koh, 2022a). Examples of this type of school include Y.K. Pao, a private boarding school in Shanghai that models itself on elite boarding schools such as Harrow or Eton. The other type includes branch campuses under the same name as UK independent schools (Wu & Koh, 2022a). Examples include Wellington College International and Dulwich College International. The main purpose of branch campuses is to replicate the successful model of the original UK school in China (Wu & Koh, 2022a).

Australian style

Australian-style schools are less numerous than other types of international school, but appear to be gaining in significance based on recent scholarship (e.g. Cutri, 2022; Dwyer, 2018; Xia, 2023). These schools typically offer the Victorian Certificate in Education (VCE) in Years 10–12 (Cutri, 2022). The VCE is a credential available to secondary school students who successfully complete Years 11 and 12 in the Australian state of Victoria and is the predominant choice for students wishing to pursue tertiary education. According to the Victorian Curriculum and Assessment Authority (VCAA), there are 24 VCE schools in China (VCAA, 2023). These schools have the same basic premise as the branded internationalised schools introduced earlier, offering a pathway to overseas higher education. VCE schools are also required to deliver the compulsory Chinese national curriculum up till Grade 9, only being able to offer the VCE from Grades 10 to 12.

Chinese internationalised schools

Unlike the previous four types of internationalised school (American, Sino-Canadian, British and Australian), which adopt the ethos and characteristics of the nation from which the curriculum is derived, Chinese internationalised schools are not branded in terms of a foreign, non-Chinese curriculum. Rather, they emphasise what might be described as 'Chinese style', while also promoting an international perspective through the adoption of international curricula (Poole, 2021). Internationalised Chinese schools have grown rapidly in the past two decades, especially in metropolitan cities such as Beijing and Shanghai (Jin, 2022). Like the previous examples, Chinese internationalised schools are regulated by the government in terms of what they teach and the need to observe certain symbolic routines, such as the raising of the national flag and the singing of the national anthem (Poole, 2021).

Chinese internationalised schools have been divided into two types: C1 (premium) and C2 (non-premium) (Bunnell & Poole, 2021). The letter 'C' is derived from Hayden and Thompson's (2013) Type C non-traditional international school, with the demarcation between C1 and C2 nuancing the types of school to be found within the Type C non-traditional category. The premium C1 type will be accredited by an external agency (such as the IBDP or International Schools Council) and will deliver an international curriculum, such as one of the four IB programmes or Cambridge's International General Certificate in Secondary Education. Premium C1 schools encompass enfranchised schools, such as the American, British, and Canadian types (Bunnell & Poole, 2021) and tend to hire teachers who hold a teaching qualification from their home countries. Non-premium schools, in contrast, will offer 'lower enrollment fees, are not accredited, nor are they members of a reputable International School association . . . many of the schools rely on the "International" name and the language of learning' (Gaskell, 2017, p. 6). The participants in this study worked in schools that straddled the C1 (premium) and C2 (non-premium) categories; they were accredited by Cambridge International Examinations, yet did not require teachers to hold formal teaching qualifications.

In order to understand how internationalised schools integrate national and international orientations (such as teaching faculty, curriculum, and school culture), international school scholars have started to make use of the burgeoning concept of 'cosmopolitan nationalism' (Maxwell et al., 2020; Wright, Ma et al., 2022; Wright, Lin et al., 2022; Yemini et al., 2023a, 2023b). According to Yemini et al. (2023a, p. 1), cosmopolitan nationalism seeks to:

> offer an analytical framework which acknowledges that at times conflicting pressures within national education structures that simultaneously promote internationalisation and a global gaze, while also wanting to remain locally relevant and a primary contributor to national projects of economic development, social cohesion and creating the 'right kinds' of citizens. Sometimes these pressures work in concert (educating future flexible workers able to compete in a global economy, who are directly involved in sustaining the development of a country), while at other times they seem to contradict one another (for instance, the possibility that creating global citizens may undercut the primary loyalties citizens have towards their own countries).

While engaging with the global is necessary for China to develop and compete on the international stage, doing so can lead to conflict over the intended role of education in responding to global concerns, on the one hand, and national priorities, on the other (Wright, Ma et al., 2022). For example, developing a global perspective might undermine students' patriotic attachment to the state. Hence the introduction of recent regulations, which has seen the 'backgrounding' of the international (e.g. restrictions on curriculum and textbooks) and the 'foregrounding' of the 'national' (e.g. Chinese national curriculum and symbolic routines) (Wu & Koh, 2022b). The resulting interplay of the global and local creates a 'confused' set of education programmes, which purport to be cosmopolitan, but in practice might be said to be rather nationalistic (Maxwell et al., 2020).

The concept of cosmopolitan nationalism is useful for understanding how, despite technically being 'international' schools, Chinese internationalised schools are fundamentally national in orientation, with the international taking on a more utilitarian function as a 'tool'. This reflects a deeply rooted *ti-yong* principle, which has informed many of China's interactions with the West. This principle might be rendered as: 'Chinese learning for essence (ti); Western learning for utility (yong)' (Fong, 2021). Applied to internationalised schooling and the concept of cosmopolitan nationalism, the *ti-yong* principle might similarly be rendered as: the national for essence; cosmopolitanism for utility. Recruiting host country national teachers is one strategy for ensuring that cosmopolitan and national perspectives are not only balanced but also configured in a way that harmonises with the *ti-yong* principle.

Departure 29

Having taken a journey through the current international school landscape, we next take another journey, this time through time, by exploring the development of the international school sector in China since its emergence in the early twentieth century to the present day – 2023. This overview situates Chinese internationalised schools within a specific historical and cultural milieu and also provides a context for understanding the emergence of host country national teachers as the new international school teacher of the future.

Disembarkation # 2: The development of the international school sector in China

Although scholars have identified a timeline of the development of the international school sector in China, there remains disagreement concerning the name, number, and date of each phase of activity. Table 2.1 summarises these phases according to Charlotte (2018), Li (2023), Jin (2022), and Deng et al. (2023). To the best of my knowledge, this book (at least in English) is the first to synthesise the different phases of international school activity. It has to be noted that there are likely more texts on the topic in Chinese, but I was unable to verify this due to my lack of proficiency in Chinese. This might be a fruitful endeavour for future collaboration between Chinese and non-Chinese scholars.

Interestingly, both Charlotte (2018) and Li (2023) use similar terms (e.g. 'embryonic'), which suggests that they both consulted the same (presumably Chinese) source(s). However, as neither author cites the source(s) from which their phases were derived, their provenance remains ambiguous. The authors also parse out each phase in terms of a ten-year time span. Curiously,

Table 2.1 Summary of the different phases of international school activity in China.

Author	Phases/years and description of each phase
Charlotte (2018)	Phase 1 (1980–1989): Embryonic stage
	Phase 2 (1990–1999): Initial growth: Exploration stage
	Phase 3 (2000–2009): Rapid development: Rising stage
	Phase 4 (2010–2019): The roaring development: Explosion stage
Li (2023)	Phase 1 (1980–1989): From nothing to something: Embryonic period
	Phase 2 (1990–1999): Preliminary development: Exploratory period
	Phase 3 (2000–2009): Rapid development: Rising period
	Phase 4 (2010–2019): Vigorous development: Explosive period
Jin (2022)	Phase 1 (1993–2009): 'Small government, big society'
	Phase 2 (2010–2015): '21 and non-21 schools'
	Phase 3 (2016–onwards): 'Chinese internationalised schools'
Deng et al. (2023)	Phase 1 (1995–2012): Introduction and support
	Phase 2 (2013–2018): Enhanced supervision and regulation
	Phase 3 (2019–onwards): Strict restriction

Li (2023), writing in 2023, does not acknowledge recent changes to the international school landscape (e.g. regulation), which suggests that a fifth phase of activity is waiting to be mapped and understood. Jin (2022) identifies three main periods of activity, with the final phase covering the emergence of internationalised schools, as well as recent regulation. While these phases are focused on Shanghai, they also mirror changes occurring in China more generally. Deng et al. (2023) also examine international schooling in Shanghai, but do so in relation to the IB and policy evolution. Changing policies towards the IB in Shanghai can be said to be a microcosm of Chinese policy towards international schooling more generally. Deng et al. (2023) also break the development of international schooling into three phases but go one step further than the other authors by describing the most recent phase (2019–onwards).

Synthesising these studies, I offer a historical overview of the international school sector in China that encompasses five phases of development: Phase 1 (1900–1949): Emergence; Phase 2 (1980–1989): Re-emergence; Phase 3 (1990–2009): International Schooling 1.0 (exploration and development); Phase 4 (2010–2019): International Schooling 2.0 (explosion and peak); and Phase 5 (2019 onwards): International Schooling 3.0 (regulation). I add two phases to the four already suggested by Li (2023): an initial embryonic stage from 1900 to 1949, which was based on Robinson and Guan (2012), and a final phase, from 2019 to the present, which was suggested by Jin (2022) and Deng et al. (2023).

Phase 1 (1900–1949): Emergence

Although international schools primarily started to emerge in China in the 1980s (Wu & Koh, 2022a), their beginnings can be traced as far back as the beginning of the twentieth century (Robinson & Guan, 2012). At that time, there was a growing need to accommodate the schooling needs of an expanding American and European expatriate population in Shanghai. An example of an international school from this time is Shanghai American School. One of the oldest international schools in China, Shanghai American School opened in 1912 in Shanghai, before closing in 1949 with the establishment of the People's Republic of China. The school would eventually reopen in 1980 and has remained in operation since that time. From 1949 to its reopening in the late 1970s/early 1980s, China had limited interactions with the West, and the fledgling international school sector stagnated and effectively ceased to exist.

Phase 2 (1980–1989): Re-emergence

International schools re-emerged in China in the 1980s as a response to the external drivers of economic globalisation and internal demand for higher-quality education that looked to the world (e.g. the West) for examples (Wu & Koh, 2022a). This process of internationalisation can be seen as part of a general state rebuilding of the education system from the 'ruins caused by the Cultural Revolution' (Huang et al., 2015, p. 25), which required every child to complete nine years of formal schooling. After the Third Plenary Session of the Eleventh Central Committee (1987), the Chinese government enacted a series of policies and laws to support the development of educational internationalisation (Qian, 2019). By 1989, there were about six international schools in China, including five schools for foreign children and one public school international department (Li, 2023).

Phase 3 (1990–2009): International Schooling 1.0 (exploration and development)

The two decades from 1990 to 2009 represented a time of deepening reform and opening up in China. According to Li (2023), this time saw rapid economic development, with the national income level steadily rising, giving birth to a growing middle class. This period could be described as 'International Schooling 1.0' as it represents the first time that the international school sector was able to develop and become accessible to an aspiring local Chinese middle class. Against a backdrop of economic development and China's re-emergence on the world stage (symbolised by its entry into the World Trade Organization in 2001 and its hosting of the Summer Olympics in Beijing in 2008), international schools started to flourish (Deng et al., 2023). The growing number of international schools was largely a bottom–up phenomenon, propelled by non-state actors providing education services which also served the state's pragmatic response to education expansion and its strategy for reducing governmental financial burdens by multiplying funding resources (Mok, 2005). At the same time, international schools were actively encouraged by the central and local governments, as they were commensurate with the prevailing logics of economic reforms and economic rationalities and external ideas and best practices to reform and innovate local education (Jin, 2022).

Phase 4 (2010–2019): International Schooling 2.0 (explosion and peak)

The period between 2010 and 2019 might be described as the 'golden age' of international schooling in China, with Jin (2022) identifying 2015 as the peak of international school activity and Li (2023, p. 11) describing this period as 'the decade of international schools in China'. The period from 2010 to 2019 might be described as 'International Schooling 2.0', as it was characterised by rapid expansion and an underlying philosophy of integration (Jin, 2022), which equated internationalisation with the fusion of both 'international' and 'national' orientations' (Poole, 2020). This integration can be found in the slogans of international schools, such as 'We integrate the best of eastern and western educational philosophy and practices' (Shanghai Arete) and 'Integrating the strengths of Chinese and Western education' (Haidian Foreign Language Education Group). The verb/noun combination of 'integrate/integration' suggested the fusion of two parts to create a new whole, which also implied a cosmopolitan openness (Wright, Lin et al., 2022) on the part of China to embrace the world.

This integration discourse was promulgated at the policy level in a seminal policy document from July 2010 titled 'The Outline of National Medium and Long-term Plan for Education Reform and Development (2010–2020)'. Although international schools were not mentioned in the document by name, the language nevertheless conveyed an openness and willingness to borrow and integrate ideas and philosophies from other countries, as illustrated by the following excerpt: 'Advanced concepts and experience in education in the world shall be assimilated to boost education reform and development at home, and to enhance the nation's global position, influence and competitiveness in the field of education' (CPC, 2010, p. 34). Global competence and international-mindedness, both of which are considered to be the outcome of an international education, might be seen as two examples of 'advanced' concepts.

Once again, the growth of the international school sector during this time can be explained by a synergy of bottom–up and top–down forces. This phase of expansion corresponds to Bunnell's (2020) notion of a 'transitionary phase' in international schooling, which is characterised by growing demand from an aspiring local middle class and growing numbers of governments enabling international schools to expand into education systems. During this period, China's standard of living continued to rise, leading to the overall quality of parents' education and outlook on education, which led them to attach more importance to education (Li, 2023). Given the fierce competition created by the Gao Kao examination (a high-stakes pre-university entrance examination), international schools emerged as an alternative to the so-called 'single plank bridge' (*du mu qiao*) schooling, which resulted in competition for limited spaces at elite universities. It is during this period that Chinese internationalised schools really started to dominate the international school market, responding to favourable policy conditions and seemingly insatiable consumer demand.

At this point, it appeared as though the international school industry would continue to expand indefinitely. However, this phase saw increasing suspicion from the government, who became alarmed at the rate at which international schools were growing. This suspicion was articulated in an internal policy document titled 'Summary of Shanghai Foreign-related Private School Policy Interpretation Conference (the Summary)' and was issued by the Shanghai Municipal Education Commission in 2016. Of most relevance to this book is the following excerpt, which is quoted from Deng et al. (2023, p. 8):

> The central government has noticed that the development of international schools is out of control and requires local governments to come up with

countermeasures and implement rectifications. China's education sovereignty has been weakened by the partial or full introduction of foreign curricula and teaching materials at the basic education stage and Chinese laws and regulations have been flouted by some private primary and secondary schools with foreign investment.

Significantly, the former integrative discourse had started to shift from one of expansion and opportunity to one that was seen to be 'out of control', potentially even undermining national interests. The government's fear would continue to grow from 2019 onwards leading to a 'reining in' (Wu & Koh, 2022b) of international schools and international curricula.

Phase 5 (2019 onwards): International Schooling 3.0 (regulation)

In the previous five years or so, there has been a subtle change in the international school landscape from 'integration' to a more China-centric discourse (Jin, 2022) that signals a 'decoupling' from the West and a drive towards self-sufficiency. Previously, integration had been understood as a form of cosmopolitan openness to international schooling (Wright, Lin et al., 2022). Now, the emphasis is not so much on 'integration', though that discourse can still be found on international school websites, but what could be described as international education with Chinese characteristics (Mansfield, 2022). International education with Chinese characteristics is designed to underscore and protect national interests. National interests include, among other things, ensuring that Chinese students receive a solid Chinese foundation during compulsory education that is 'rooted' in Chinese culture, which can lead to the development of a Chinese identity.

Interestingly, the metaphor of 'roots' recurs throughout internationalised school mission statements, as illustrated in the following examples found online:

> Rooted in Chinese culture and values, who are prepared to be actively engaged citizens in the global community.
> (Tsinghua University High School International)

> We believe in building the best true international bilingual school on deep Chinese roots.
> (BIBS)

> Competitive and Successful Life-long Learners Deeply Rooted in traditional Chinese Culture.
> (Pinghe)

Significantly, the metaphor of 'roots' echoes the wider political discourse in China, appearing to ape the rhetoric of China's leader, Xi Jing Ping, which emphasises the centrality of China:

> Education in China must reflect the unique characteristics of China and be adapted to the country's context. It has to be rooted in China while building bridges connecting with foreign lands, and it must keep abreast with the times and be forward-thinking.
>
> (Xi, 2022, p. 9)

'Rooted' conveys a sense of firm attachment. The image of 'bridge building' meanwhile suggests that interaction with the international community is still important for China, but it should be done on China's terms – that is, China takes what it needs in order to fulfil its long-term policy of self-rejuvenation and common prosperity and to remain free of cultural pollution.

This change in discourse – from integration to decoupling – informs government regulation of the international school industry in China. Recent regulation of the international school market in China has sought to 'rein in' (Wu & Koh, 2022b) the international by emphasising existing regulations, as well as introducing new rules, such as restrictions on curriculum, admissions, and ownership (Jones et al., 2021). For example, international schools catering for Chinese students now require Chinese students to study the national curriculum for the nine years of compulsory education from elementary to junior high school either alongside or instead of international programmes (Wright, Ma et al., 2022). Recent regulations also require students to undertake national curriculum courses during high school, such as moral education, as well as observe symbolic routines, such as singing the national anthem (Poole, 2021).

Wright, Lin et al.'s (2022) content analysis of government documents and state media helps to shed light on recent regulation. Although the paper focuses on the IB, much of their analysis resonates with international schools more generally and internationalised schools (or private bilingual schools) more specifically. According to the authors, government policy and state media have highlighted Chinese identity, commercialisation, and inequality as issues that require attention through regulation. Deng et al. (2023) also make a similar argument, considering the government's actions to be a response to the potential undermining of sovereignty, cultural identity, and educational equity due to the expansion of the private international school sector.

In terms of Chinese cultural identity, international schools are considered to have become 'too internationalised, or more specifically Westernised, and thus detached from the goals of instilling a collective memory, pride, and patriotic feelings for the Chinese nation' (Wright, Lin et al., 2022, p. 7). From the perspective of commercialisation, the government has become concerned that internationalised schools have been 'corrupted by a profit-orientation, especially through the entrance of foreign investors, that distorted the role of schools in educating the next generation' (Wright, Lin et al., 2022, p. 7). Finally, internationalised schools are seen as problematic due to concerns stemming from a commitment that international education should not be restricted to a socio-economic elite and 'affluent families should not be able to use economic means to enable their children to "optout" of compulsory national education and gain educational advantages' (Wright, Lin et al., 2022, p. 8).

From a Western perspective, these regulations have largely been depicted in terms of a crackdown (Ho-Him & Olcott, 2022) or in related terms, such as 'prohibiting' (The Standard, 2021) and 'barring' (Reuters, 2021). While many have framed International Schooling 3.0 in terms of the end of an era (e.g. Chan & Olcott, 2022; The Standard, 2021), others (e.g. Mansfield, 2022) have adopted a more pragmatic outlook. From the perspective of Chinese policymakers (as well as some educational actors), these changes are likely to be perceived more positively as necessary reforms to an out-of-control sector, rife with commercialisation and inequality (Wright, Lin et al., 2022).

Perhaps what we are now seeing in the most recent phase of International Schooling 3.0 is a rejection of, and decoupling from, a global form of international schooling that emphasises universal values and democratic education and, instead, the sanitising of the international, leading to the construction of an 'international' that is now commensurate with a China-centric discourse that no longer strives to cultivate integration but seeks to achieve what might best be described as cultural autarchy – rooted in China, but building bridges with the West only insofar as it serves an agenda of national rejuvenation. To put it more poetically, whereas previously the 'West wind had overpowered the East wind' (Tan & Chua, 2015), the most recent phase of International Schooling 3.0 is seeing the resurgence of the East wind. Recalling the underlying framework of this book – China as method/China as global method – this move towards growing nationalism and autarchic retreat from the global is by no means unique to China but needs to be understood in terms of global linkages (Franceschini & Loubere, 2022), which has seen similar occurrences in the wake of the global pandemic and growing geopolitical tensions created by the war in Ukraine and other regional conflicts.

Given these changes, it might be tempting to view International Schooling 3.0 as inherently unwelcomed, as it has seen a 'reining in' (Wu & Koh, 2022b) and re-tooling of the international in China, which could be said to have resulted in international schools becoming diluted (Poole & Bunnell, 2023) or perhaps too far removed from the original model of the traditional international school (Hayden & Thompson, 2013). However, with the notion of China as method firmly in mind, adopting a more China-centric perspective allows a more nuanced picture to emerge. Rather than insisting on some form of 'pure' international school (i.e. traditional international schools), it may be more realistic to think of international schools (catering for Chinese students) in China as morphing into a new form.

In a previous paper (Poole, 2020), I described this new school as the 'prototypical school of the future'. However, on reflection, I realise that this type of school was predicated upon the notion of 'integration' or 'dovetailing' (Poole & Bunnell, 2023), which, while consonant with the underlying integrative philosophy of 'International Schooling 2.0' is now, in a time of 'International Schooling 3.0', anachronistic, perhaps even taboo or subversive. The new archetypical school of a post-regulatory landscape can no longer be the Chinese internationalised school as initially conceived, but rather something that reflects a discourse of 'roots' and 'bridges' – something like what Mansfield (2022) describes as the 'internationally-facing' school – that is, schools 'rooted' in China but strategically positioned to 'build bridges' (Xi, 2022) to the rest of the world. Pearce (2023) has also offered the emerging concept of the 'internationally-national school' which corresponds to the notion of the internationally facing school. According to Pearce (2023), the internationally national school is one that aligns itself with one or more nationalities; may or may not use an international curriculum, but which is underpinned by a national curriculum; incorporates an international dimension; and is open for enrolment to citizens of any country.

It is in this new restrictive phase of International Schooling 3.0 that I situate my exploration of host country national teachers' motivations and mobilities. While this new landscape will be a loss for many, including expatriate teachers who, it is reported, are starting to leave China in the wake of the COVID-19-related policies (Hall, 2022; Shazal, 2022), it may offer 'opportunities' for those who have remained on the margins, in the wings, waiting patiently for their turn to take the stage:

> The shortage of Western teachers is hastening what was already a growing trend towards the localisation of international staffing, and more and more of the 1,000-plus international curriculum schools in China will seek to use Chinese bilinguals, many returning from living or studying overseas, to deliver their curriculum. This is in no way a bad thing. In fact, it may well serve as the next stage in the altering of what had previously been a rather neo-paternal intervention in Chinese education by the Western teaching community.
>
> (Mansfield, 2022)

The returnee teachers that Mansfield writes about are well suited to interpret and enact an 'internationally-national' ethos, something which expatriate teachers are either likely to misunderstand or actively resist. Against a backdrop of 'International Schooling 3.0', the host country national teacher is emerging as a key educational actor. As Mansfield argues, host country national teachers are a good fit for a regulated landscape, which has changed from being internationalised to 'internationally-facing'. Host country national teachers are also likely to replace expatriate teachers who, as mentioned earlier, have started to leave

China, although it is yet to be seen if the lifting of pandemic restrictions in early 2023 will entice teachers back. Host country national teachers might thus be seen as 'international school teachers 3.0' – the new international school teacher for a post-regulated landscape. As such, understanding host country national teachers' experiences will become increasingly essential for a range of actors, including school leaders, researchers, and policymakers. Despite now occupying a significant position in the new international school landscape, host country national teachers still remain under-researched, under-theorised, and under-represented. What kind of host country teachers are there? Why do these teachers join international schools? What experiences do they bring with them? These questions will be answered in Chapter 3.

Disembarkation# 3: Meeting the participants

Having provided the context for understanding host country national teachers' motivations for working in private international schools, it is time to make the final disembarkation and meet the participants and learn about their teaching contexts. The reader is asked to imagine that they have disembarked and have been led into a school assembly hall. The participants have prepared a short presentation where they will introduce themselves and their school. They will continue their stories in Chapter 3, where they will talk about their journeys into international school teaching in China. In order to make the participants' biographies more vivid and engaging, I have decided to dramatise them by combining extracts from the interviews with my own words. Therefore, while taking some artistic licence in how I present the participants' biographies, they remain rooted in the participants' lived experiences as expressed during their interviews. I also denote the participants' gender, as it is not always discernible from their names and will become significant in the following chapter.

Without further ado, I would like to first introduce Ru (male):

> Hello everyone. My name is Ru. I'm in my late twenties. I currently work in a small international school in Beijing called North China International School or NCIS. I say school, but it is more like a department or centre, as it occupies only one floor of the university it is located in. NCIS offers the Cambridge IGCSE and A Level, and the students are all Chinese. I teach Computer Science and have been working in the school for about six months. I also spent some time in the US, where I studied and worked, but decided to return to China. The main purpose of my return to China is to serve China. I love China more than anything, and I must come back. You know, in Chinese, people who return to the Motherland are referred to as 'sea turtles' or *haigui*. So I guess you could say that I am a sea turtle! My passion is teaching, I think I must be a teacher no matter the salary. I look forward to sharing my story with you in Chapter 3.

Thank you, Ru. Next up is Shu (female):

> Nice to meet you all. My name is Shu. I'm in my early thirties and currently work in Central China International School or CCIS for short. It's a K–12 school in Shanghai and offers the IGCSE and the IBDP. There are an equal mix of foreign and host country national teachers here, so I'd say it is a proper international school. I teach high-school and middle-school students who struggle with their English. I call it 'Dummy's English' because I really want to be a proper English teacher. Anyway, I wanted to be a public school teacher, but I encountered many problems, so I ended up working in a number of training centres and then, finally, in CCIS. I'll tell you more about it in Chapter 3. It's a complicated story, so you'd better brush up on your Chinese. I suggest you preview some key concepts, like *hukou* and also do a bit of reading on the teaching profession in China. I believe Adam will also provide you with some background information as well.

Thank you, Shu. I will definitely have something to say about the *hukou* system and the teaching profession in Chapter 3. Now I would like to introduce everyone to Jin (male):

> Hey everyone. My name is Jin and I currently teach chemistry at Southern Diversity, or SD for short, which is located in medium-sized city about two hours from Shanghai. My school offers Cambridge's IGCSE and A Level. The school has over 400 teachers, but the high school section I work in has 40 host country national teachers and only two expatriate teachers. It's hard to recruit foreign teachers right now because of the pandemic. Like Shu, I started my teaching career in private training schools. At that time, training institutions were still hot, so finding a job was very easy. Then after two years of work, I had the opportunity to work in an international school in Beijing. However, the *hukou* system made finding a school for my children really difficult, so I decided to move with my family to this new school, where things are a lot easier.

That was very nice. It seems that the *hukou* system is something of a headache for host country national teachers. Now I would like to introduce Ying (female):

> Hello everyone. I'm Ying, and I teach Chinese as a foreign language. Like Jin, I also work in Southern Diversity. I have been in the international field for a long time. I first taught Chinese as a foreign language in a university for about ten years but decided to work at SD as it gave me access to a lot of quality educational resources for my two children. You know, the educational resources of children are a very important consideration for mums. I have to think about the different education I can provide for my

children. I also happen to live near this school. This is why I have never left my job in this school because I have a lot of comprehensive considerations. So I think of myself as a '*xiaokang* parent'. Don't worry, Adam will explain what it means in Chapter 3. Oh, I'd like to add a few things about Southern Diversity that Jin missed. So, a lot of the teachers here don't have formal teaching qualifications or have passed the National Teacher Certificate Examination. You need the National Teacher Certificate Examination to work in a public school, but as we are private international school teachers being qualified isn't a problem. At least for the time being. Who knows how things will turn out after the new regulations, right?

Thank you. Thank you. Yes, I definitely have a lot to say about *xiaokang* parents. Finally, I'd like to ask Gang (male) to come up and say a few words:

Hi! My name is Gang. I also work at Southern Diversity and currently teach Physics. One final thing about the school that Ying and Jin forgot to mention is the average age of our teachers is between 30 and 35 years old. Half of our teachers have international study experience and since they have experienced it first hand, they have a deeper understanding of international education. I think it's a coincidence that I entered an international school. Like Ru, I came back from studying abroad and there was a famous school near our home, and then an international school opened in this famous school. Then, like Ying, I thought that my children would go to school and work closer later, so I planned to go to this international school department for a job interview. After all, it's on the doorstep, and then I went, and then I tried it, and then I found that everything was okay. However, I decided to move to Southern Diversity about three months ago, so I am new here. I think it is also okay, and it can also solve the problem of my children's education. The welfare benefits are also better.

Thank you all. Oh, before I forget, I should also invite Mei (female) to the stage. She works at a school called South China International School (SCIS). As some of the teachers from this school will also be featured in Chapter 3, you will of course want to know something about their school. Welcome, Mei:

Hi everyone. I teach English at SCIS. The school is a 'typical private school' located approximately three hours' drive from Shanghai, but it is very remote, with some of our teachers describing it as 'rural'. Like the other schools mentioned, SCIS offers the IGCSE and A Level. The school has a total of 73 students, who are divided into five classes: two Grade 10 classes (30 students), two Grade 11 classes (30 students), and one Grade 12 class (13 students). There are 15 teachers and seven administrators. Of the 15 teachers, four are expatriates, with the remaining being host country national teachers. In Chapter 3, you will hear from us SCIS teachers from time to time, so don't forget us!

Conclusion

This chapter provided the reader with three contexts (or disembarkations) for understanding the emergence of host country national teachers in China. The first disembarkation involved a stroll through the different types of international school in China. As the participants worked in a specific type of international school – what I describe as a Chinese internationalised school – it was necessary to consider how these schools are compare to other types of international school. The second disembarkation saw us taking a virtual historical tour through the development of international schooling in China. This helped to show the reader how the emergence of host country national teachers is the product of China's changing relationship with the West and migration practices, which have seen increased return migration of overseas Chinese. The third disembarkation involved meeting the participants, who shared information about their biographies and schools.

The next chapter will explore the participants' journeys into international schooling. While their motivation is the primary focus of analysis, it will also be necessary to consider the related issue of their mobilities. As the reader will see, motivation and mobility cannot easily be parsed in the study of international school teachers as one invokes the other.

References

Alexander, I. (2023). Student perspectives of academic discourse socialization in British Columbia offshore schools in China. *Journal of Language, Identity & Education*, 1–15.

Bunnell, T. (2020). The continuous growth and development of "international schooling": The notion of a "transitionary phase". *Compare: A Journal of Comparative and International Education*, *50*(5), 764–768.

Bunnell, T. (2022). Moving from elite international schools to elite (ish) universities: The pathway leading to Toronto rather than Harvard. *Educational Studies*, 1–13.

Bunnell, T., & Atkinson, C. (2020). Exploring enduring employment discrimination in favour of British and American teachers in "traditional international schools". *Journal of Research in International Education*, *19*(3), 251–267.

Bunnell, T., & Poole, A. (2021). *Precarity and insecurity in international schooling: New realities and new visions*. Emerald.

Cao, R. Q. (2021). International schools: A good with special value for Chinese Middle Class. *Advances in Social Science, Education and Humanities Research*, *631*, 962–967.

Central Party Committee (CPC) and State Council. (2010). *Outline of national medium and long-term plan for education reform and development (2010–2020)*. www.moe.gov.cn/srcsite/A01/s7048/201007/t20100729_171904.html.

Chan, H., & Olcott, E. (2022). China's international school sector threatened by COVID and crackdown. *Financial Times*. www.ft.com/content/2ae60e40-2c95-47ad-9c97-47ef643fad80

Charlotte, C. (2018). *1980–2019: A brief history of international education in China*. https://tech.ifeng.com/c/7fq2Pc39Oxp

Cutri, J. E. (2022). *The localisation of Australian elite education within China: A case-study of various social actors' experiences at a Sino-Australian senior school* [Doctoral thesis, Monash University]. https://doi.org/10.26180/21323604.v1

Delval, A. S. (2022). Legitimising an unusual choice abroad for privileged students: Swiss hospitality management schools as "refuge schools". *British Journal of Sociology of Education, 43*(8), 1216–1232.

Deng, L., Wu, S. Y., Chen, Z. M., & Peng, Z. M. (2023). Threat or necessity: An analysis of the development of International Baccalaureate education in Shanghai. *Educational Review*. https://doi.org/10.1080/00131911.2023.2182761

Dwyer, N. (2018). Crossing the river by feeling the stones: Establishing an Australian school in China. *Independence, 43*(1), 60–61. http://doi.org/10.3316/aeipt.219951

EDA. (2023). *List of American curriculum international schools in China*. *Education Destination Asia*. https://educationdestinationasia.com/schools/american-curriculum/china?order_by=name,asc&page=2

Fong, E. T. Y. (2021). *English in China: Language, identity and culture*. Routledge.

Franceschini, I., & Loubere, N. (2022). *Global China as method*. Cambridge University Press.

Gaskell, R. (2017). Potential international school growth for the Philippines. *Linked In*. www.linkedin.com/pulse/potential-international-school-growth-philippines-richard-gaskell

Hall, C. (2022). China's international schools hit by exodus of teachers dejected by COVID curbs. *Reuters*. www.reuters.com/world/china/chinas-international-schools-hit-by-exodus-teachers-dejected-by-covid-curbs-2022-05-20/

Hayden, M., & Thompson, J. (2013). International schools: Antecedents, current issues and metaphors for the future. In R. Pearce (Ed.), *International education and schools: Moving beyond the first 40 years* (pp. 3–24). Bloomsbury Academic.

Ho-him, C, & Olcott, E. (2022). China's international school sector threatened by Covid and crackdown. *Financial Times*. https://www.ft.com/content/2ae60e40-2c95-47ad-9c97-47ef643fad80

Huang, Z., Wang, T., & Li, X. (2015). The political dynamics of educational changes in China. *Policy Futures in Education, 14*(1), 24–41.

Jin, J. (2022). Ambivalent governance and the changing role of the state: Understanding the rise of international schools in Shanghai through the lens of policy networks. *International Journal of Educational Research, 114*, 102004.

Jones, P., Isaacson, J., & Morgan-McDermott, G. (2021). *A new regulatory landscape for international schools in China*. Farrer & Co. www.farrer.co.uk/news-and-insights/a-new-regulatory-landscape-for-international-schools-in-china/

Kim, H., & Mobrand, E. (2019). Stealth marketisation: How international school policy is quietly challenging education systems in Asia. *Globalisation, Societies and Education, 17*(3), 310–323.

Lee, M., & Wright, E. (2016). Moving from elite international schools to the world's elite universities: A critical perspective. *International Journal of Comparative Education and Development, 18*(2), 120–136.

Li, J. (2023). *International school policy development: Insights from China*. Springer Nature.

Ma, K. X. (2023). Exploring the changing pathway to cultivating an elite "international" child in China. *ESSC, 2022*, 1–4. https://doi.org/10.1051/shsconf/202315704008

Ma, Y., & Wright, E. (2021). Outsourced concerted cultivation: International schooling and educational consulting in China. *International Studies in Sociology of Education*, 1–23.

Mansfield, D. (2022). How reforms have affected British schools in China. *TES Magazine*. www.tes.com/magazine/analysis/specialist-sector/how-reforms-have-affected-british-schools-china

Maxwell, C., Yemini, M., Engel, L., & Lee, M. (2020). Cosmopolitan nationalism in the cases of South Korea, Israel and the US. *British Journal of Sociology of Education, 41*(6), 845–858.

Mok, K. H. (2005). Riding over socialism and global capitalism: Changing education governance and social policy paradigms in post-Mao China. *Comparative Education, 41*(2), 217–242.

Pearce, S. (2023). Internationally-national schools: A critical review of this developing sector and the frameworks that define international schools. *Research in Comparative and International Education*. http://doi.org/10.1177/17454999231167948

Poole, A. (2017). Interpreting and implementing the IB learner profile in an internationalised school in China: A shift of focus from the "profile as text" to the "lived profile". *Journal of Research in International Education, 16*(3), 248–264.

Poole, A. (2020). Decoupling Chinese internationalised schools from normative constructions of the international school. *Compare: A Journal of Comparative and International Education, 50*(3), 447–454.

Poole, A. (2021). *International teachers' lived experiences: Examining internationalised schooling in Shanghai*. Springer Nature.

Poole, A., & Bunnell, T. (2023). Diluting, decoupling, and dovetailing: Considering new metaphors for understanding the changing international school landscape in China. *Journal of Research in International Education, 22*(1), 3–19. https://doi.org/10.1177/14752409231160710

Poole, A., Liujinya, Y., & Yue, S. (2022). "We're away from everything": Understanding the struggles faced by internationalized schools in non-urban contexts in China. *Sage Open, 12*(1), 21582440221081026.

Qian, R. (2019). A discussion of the situation, problems and potential solutions of developing international education through implementing international division in Chinese Normal model high school. In *1st international symposium on education, culture and social sciences (ECSS 2019)* (pp. 408–420). Atlantis Press.

Reuters. (2021). China bars foreign curricula, ownership in some private schools. *Reuters*. www.reuters.com/world/china/china-bars-foreign-curriculum-ownership-some-private-schools-2021-05-17/

Robinson, J., & Guan, X. (2012). The changing face of international education in China. *On the Horizon, 2*(4), 305–312.

Shazal, S. (2022). Teachers leave Shanghai amid ongoing lockdown – How will this affect int'l students? *Study International*. www.studyinternational.com/news/teachers-leaving-chinas-schools/

Smart Shanghai. (2021). Tuition fees and costs of international schools in Shanghai. *Smart Shanghai*. www.smartshanghai.com/articles/education/inside-education-tuition-fees-and-costs-of-international-schools-in-shanghai

The Standard. (2021). China prohibits foreign curriculum in schools and foreign ownership. *The Standard.* www.thestandard.com.hk/breaking-news/section/3/172376/China-prohibits-foreign-curriculum-in-schools-and-foreign-ownership

Sun, Y. (2014). *The study of internationalization of Chinese higher education (1983–2013)* [PhD thesis, East China Normal University]. http://cdmd.cnki.com.cn/Article/CDMD-10269-1014322185.htm.

Tan, C., & Chua, C. S. (2015). Education policy borrowing in China: Has the West wind overpowered the East wind? *Compare: A Journal of Comparative and International Education, 45*(5), 686–704.

Tang, S. (2004). *The questing and transcendence of secondary school education.* People's Education Press.

Tang, X. (2014). Some thinking of developing international class in normal high school. *Journal of Educational Development, 4*(9), 21–24.

Tarc, P., & Mishra Tarc, A. (2015). Elite international schools in the Global South: Transnational space, class relationalities and the "middling" international schoolteacher. *British Journal of Sociology of Education, 36*(1), 34–52.

VCAA. (2023). The VCE in China. *VCAA.* www.vcaa.vic.edu.au/About-us/International/China/Pages/China.aspx

Wang, F. (2017). Canadian offshore schools in China: A comparative policy analysis. *Journal of Education Policy, 32*(5), 523–541.

Wright, E., Lin, C., & Lu, J. (2022). The turning tide of the International Baccalaureate in China: When global dreams meet national priorities. *Globalisation, Societies and Education,* 1–14.

Wright, E., Ma, Y., & Auld, E. (2022). Experiments in being global: The cosmopolitan nationalism of international schooling in China. *Globalisation, Societies and Education, 20*(2), 236–249.

Wright, E., & Mulvey, B. (2022). The promised capitals of international high school programmes and the global field of higher education: The case of Shenzhen, China. *Journal of Research in International Education, 21*(2), 87–104.

Wu, W. (2020). The rise of international schools in China-critical perspectives on trends and issues. *CIES.* https://cies2020.org/wp-content/uploads/WenxiWu-Theriseofinternationalschoolsin China-criticalperspectivesontrendsandissues-copy.pdf

Wu, W., & Koh, A. (2022a). Being "international" differently: A comparative study of transnational approaches to international schooling in China. *Educational Review, 74*(1), 57–75.

Wu, W., & Koh, A. (2022b). Reining in the international: How state and society localised international schooling in China. *British Journal of Educational Studies,* 1–20.

Wu, X., & Tarc, P. (2021). Chinese international students in a Canadian private secondary school: Becoming flexible citizens? *Compare: A Journal of Comparative and International Education, 51*(6), 901–919.

Xi, J. P. (2022). *Understanding Xi Jinping's educational philosophy.* Foreign Language Teaching and Research Press.

Xia, Q. (2023). *The multiple indicators in creating an effective private international school in the context of China: A case study of two secondary schools offering Australian courses* [Doctoral thesis, Monash University]. https://doi.org/10.26180/21893112.v1

Yemini, M., Maxwell, C., Wright, E., Engel, L., & Lee, M. (2023a). Call for papers: Cosmopolitan nationalism: Analytical potentials and challenges. *Discourse: Studies in the Cultural Politics of Education*, 1–2.

Yemini, M., Maxwell, C., Wright, E., Engel, L., & Lee, M. (2023b). Cosmopolitan nationalism as an analytical lens: Four articulations in education policy. *Policy Futures in Education*. https://doi.org/10.1177/14782103231168672

Young, N. A. (2018). Departing from the beaten path: International schools in China as a response to discrimination and academic failure in the Chinese educational system. *Comparative Education, 54*(2), 159–180.

3 Arrival

Considering the motivations and mobilities of Returners, Reachers, and Remainers

Introduction

As established in Chapter 1, there is a burgeoning literature which explores expatriate teachers' motivations and mobilities, but comparatively little has been written about host country national teachers. In order to address this gap, this chapter develops the theorisation of host country national teachers by considering their journeys into international schooling. Specifically, this chapter explores the lived experiences of host country national teachers by considering their motivations and, to a lesser extent, mobilities. In order to help me with this endeavour, I return to and expand a typology previously sketched in a paper of mine titled 'More than interchangeable "local" teachers' (Poole, 2022). That paper concluded by identifying three types of host country national teacher in China, whom I labelled Returners, Reachers, and Remainers.

The rest of this chapter considers each type – Returners, Reachers, and Remainers – in turn. In keeping with the metaphor of the journey, the reader is asked to imagine that the author is giving a virtual tour through the participants' lived experiences. From time to time, the participants will be asked to take the floor and share their personal recollections in the form of indented quotation blocks. For the rest of the time, the author will function as a tour guide of sorts, offering additional insights and relevant conceptual and background information so the reader can understand and interpret the participants' experiences.

Ru will take the stage first to talk about his experiences as a Returner teacher and how he went from starting his own IT company in the United States to working as a computer science teacher in an international school in Beijing. The concepts of *guoji rencai* (international talents), *haigui* (sea turtle), and international capital will be used to make sense of the experiences of Returners like Ru. While Ru's story forms the basis of the theorisation of the Returner label, participants from SCIS will also take the stage to contextualise Ru's experiences and create points of triangulation. Shu will then share her experiences as a Reacher teacher and explain how her frustrated attempts to become a public school teacher led her to becoming an English-language-support assistant in an international school. In order to illuminate Shu's experiences, I offer background information related to the teaching profession in China, as well as the *hukou* (household registration) system. Jin will also take the stage to share his experiences as a Reacher teacher. Finally, Ying and Gang will close out the virtual tour of host country national teachers' journeys into international schooling by sharing why working in a school close to their families is of strategic importance to them as part of an aspiring, yet precariously positioned, middle class. The concept of immobility and *xiaokang* parents will be used to nuance the concept of the middle class which, as a Western concept, does not quite fit the social and political idiosyncrasies of the Chinese context.

Returners

Returners have studied or worked overseas and strategically use international school teaching to make up for a lack of *guanxi*/social capital. Before exploring Ru's journey into international schooling, it is necessary to consider notions of *rencai*, *guoji rencai*, and *haigui*, as they play a significant part in understanding the experiences of Returners.

Guoji rencai

Rencai refers to high levels of human capital typically measured as the percentage of the population with a bachelor's degree or higher educational attainment. Talent workers are highly valued in China because of the clear links between human capital, economic development, prosperity, and economic growth (MacLachlan & Gong, 2022). *Guoji rencai*, meanwhile, translates as 'international' or 'global talent'. Traditionally, *guoji rencai* referred to highly skilled foreign workers who were urgently needed by China in order to maintain and enhance the country's status in the knowledge-based global economy (Miao et al., 2022). Despite initiating numerous policies aimed at settling international professionals in China (such as the Thousand Talents Scheme and relaxing visa requirements for urgently needed talents), China still lags behind other countries, such as Japan and Singapore (CCG, 2017), with expatriates comprising only about 0.06 per cent of the total population (Bickenbach & Liu, 2022).

Increasingly, *guoji rencai* has come to be applied to Chinese citizens who have studied or worked overseas and whom the government desire to return to China to serve the motherland (Qian, 2007). These returnees are urgently required, among other things, to promote sci-tech progress; enhance China's contact with the world; and expand China's exchanges relating to international politics, economies, societies, and cultures (Qian, 2007). The Chinese government has emphasised the recruitment of high-skilled returnees and included this as an essential strategic step that has been addressed in three national middle- and long-term development plans: the National Plan for Medium- and Long-Term Scientific and Technological Development (2006–2020); National Plan for Medium- and Long-Term Human Resources Development (2010–2020); and National Plan for Medium- and Long-Term Education Reform and Development (2010–2020) (Hao & Welch, 2012).

Haigui

Haigui (sea turtles) is a colloquial term given to returning high-skilled, experienced graduates (i.e. *guoji rencai*) who have studied and/or worked overseas (Hao & Welch, 2012). *Haigui* literally translates as 'returnees from overseas' but is also a homonym that sounds like 'sea turtles' (Zweig & Han, 2010). As a consequence of an expanding middle class and the liberalisation of overseas student recruitment beginning in the mid-2000s, the number of Chinese students moving abroad for bachelor's and master's degrees has dramatically increased in the past 20 years (Du et al., 2021). Between 2015 and 2018, the number of returnees increased from about 409,100 to 519,400, or by roughly 26.9 per cent (Zou, 2019). Internationally educated graduates (*guoji rencai*), particularly the high-skilled from world-leading universities, often have key advantages over domestic graduates in terms of seeking employment (Hao & Welch, 2012). For example, returnees bring with them 'international capital', which can be understood as a subset of Bourdieu's cultural capital (1990). According to Maire (2022, p. 1176), international capital is theorised as:

> existing in institutionalised, embodied and objectified' states'. Some forms of multilingualism or experiences of international mobility would be examples of its embodied state while cultural goods symbolising international or intercultural knowledge or identities would be examples of its objectified state.

In relation to *haigui* Chinese, embodied international capital might take the form of enhanced English language skills or intercultural awareness. Objectified international capital might refer to international qualifications, such as master's degrees or PhDs, which exert symbolic power signalling a candidate's abilities to potential employers (Du et al., 2021).

Despite their international capital, research (Du et a., 2021; Hao & Welch, 2012) suggests that many returnees will struggle to find a job on their return, often settling for salaries below their (some would argue unrealistic) expectations. This situation has been attributed to the rapid increase in high-skilled returnees (Hao & Welch, 2012), a decrease in the quality of people going overseas (Zweig & Han, 2010), and an improvement in the quality of domestic graduates and domestic higher education (Du et al., 2021). This phenomenon has led to many returnees 'waiting for a job' (*dai ye*). While they were once the venerated and valuable 'sea turtles', returnees find themselves becoming 'sea weed' (*hai dai*), another homonym for 'overseas returnees waiting for work' (Du et al., 2021).

Ru's journey (or 'I love China more than anything, and I must come back')

When I interviewed Ru in 2021, he had left behind a number of failed entrepreneurial endeavours in the United States and China, as well as a high-paying job in the IT industry to work in an international school. Understanding how and why he moved from IT to international school teaching (as well as from the United States back to China) offers an insight into the experiences of *haigui* who may view working in an international school as a way of escaping from the 'sea weed' (*hai dai*) of precarity. Ru's case also offers evidence of the entrepreneurial spirit of overseas returnees (Xiao & Wang, 2022) and the issues that arise when they attempt to 'make it' in China and invariably fail due to the lack of necessary *guanxi* (i.e. connections/social capital) due to being outside of the country and effectively being left behind by their domestic peers who are better placed to build the necessary connections to get their foot in the door of employment after graduation. Ru's experiences, while by no means representative, are offered as evidence to support Mansfield's (2022) assertion that *haigui* are turning to international school teaching in part because their international capital in both symbolic and embodied forms is highly valued by non-traditional international schools.

The call of the American Dream

Like many of his peers, Ru was lured to the United States by the promise of the 'American Dream'. After gaining a degree from the University of California, he had planned to remain in the United States for the long term in order to set up his own IT business and perhaps even settle down. As he put it, 'Why I decided to go the US? I wanted to work there for a long time. Like maybe get married'. Like many of the participants, Ru did not study teaching in university. This was echoed by the other participants who had studied or worked overseas and then returned to China. For example, Zixin (SCIS) majored in tourism and hospitality management, while Chang (SCIS) 'didn't study teaching when I was a college student, but after graduation, I worked in a Confucius Institute in Myanmar for three years as a Chinese teacher'.

Although Ru had only been in the United States for a few years, he was soon able to set up his own IT company, focusing on game development with the help of two Chinese classmates:

> But, why do game development? I'm really interested in that. And I feel enthusiastic. I feel I'm very good at it. I do technical things. I programme

very good. So I can be an IT director or a CTO in a company. So suddenly, I actually had my own company. I started a company with two Chinese people, who were my classmates. I was very focused on that.

Ru's decision to set up his own company is an example of the entrepreneurial spirit that is often associated with *guoji rencai* who have studied and worked overseas (Du et al., 2021). The adverb 'suddenly' gives a sense of the speed with which Ru set up his own company, while the adverb 'actually' gives the sense that Ru could not quite believe that he had his own company – perhaps it had just been a dream, but now it had become a reality.

It seemed at this point that the American Dream was easily within reach. However, Ru's initial success was to be short-lived:

But after a year, the market changed. I was working on mobile games. I programmed several relaxing games. They are just very complex games. It's very funny. I suppose it's funny. But they did not sell very well in the market. We had very high technology people here so my background is computer science, and all my classmates are very good at programming. But we don't know the market. We don't have sales, so we don't know what is good for the trending of the market. So there is no investment, so I didn't have the chance to stay in America.

Although Ru and his friends had the technical skills needed to create a product, they did not have the necessary insider knowledge of the American games' industry to market and sell their product. As such, they struggled to make a profit and the company was forced to close, resulting in Ru leaving America and returning to China.

The call of the Chinese Dream

Ru's decision to return to China was not just influenced by the failure of his IT company but also by the 'call of the homeland' (Jiang, 2021):

The main purpose of my return to China is to serve China. Although I have many years of work experience in the United States and I have already achieved the position of CTO, I don't think the United States is a good country. I love China more than anything, and I must come back.

While Ru's negative perception of the United States may have been the result of his difficult experiences, it may also have been influenced by Chinese government propaganda. Ru's interviews indicated a patriotic attachment to China, which compelled him to return. Increasingly, many Chinese overseas students are choosing to pursue the Chinese Dream (*Zhong Guo Meng*). In Ru's case, it appears as though he set out to pursue the American Dream, but after failing to attain it, he heeded the call of the homeland and followed the Chinese Dream instead.

The Chinese Dream was first mentioned in a speech by Chinese leader Xi Jing Ping in 2012 and ostensibly refers to building a moderately prosperous society and realising national rejuvenation. As part of this dream, younger Chinese, like Ru, go out into the world to become *guoji rencai* and return as *haigui*, bringing back with them advanced skills and knowledge in order to contribute to the project of national rejuvenation. As Jiang (2021, p. 34) very elegantly puts it,

> [T]he seemingly contradictory existence of the transnational desire for Western education and rising nationalist sentiments work jointly in the neoliberal market economy to build entrepreneurial individuals, who are expected to contribute to China's economic growth as well as political rejuvenation.

However, some Western commentators (e.g. BBC, 2013; Ibrahim, 2020) have noted that behind the seemingly positive idea of prosperity and progress lies a more insidious motive: to make China the world's dominant power. For these commentators, patriotism has become a strategy for the Chinese government to address the issue of 'brain-drain'. Here we see an example of *guoji rencai* (international talents) being recalled to China in order to strengthen the nation through their entrepreneurial and international skills. However, as Ru's narrative will show, years spent away from China can make it difficult for Returners to reintegrate into Chinese society and get a foothold in the labour market.

Waking up from the dream

Despite having high hopes to seize the Chinese Dream and realise his entrepreneurial ambitions in a country he grew up in and loved, Ru once again struggled to set up another games company on his return:

> Then I found I could start a business in Shanghai. Then I went to Shanghai. It was even worse than America. Yeah, I don't know the reason. I didn't find a good partner. So I had a circle in America, in a city called Wyoming, and also my classmates. But in Shanghai, I know nobody and I just lost a little bit of my confidence.

Ru may have selected Shanghai as a strategic re-entry point as it is the most cosmopolitan city in China (which would value his international capital) and is a key destination for returnee entrepreneurs, with, as of 2021, approximately 220,000 returnees working or running businesses there (Zhou, 2021). Ru's passing reference to not being able to find a 'good partner' suggests that he did not have the necessary *guanxi* (connections) to get his business off the ground on his return. Ironically, Ru may have been in a more advantageous position in the United States, as he was surrounded by a close circle of Chinese classmates; however, on his return to China, he was unable to rely on this *guanxi* network. As Ru was from Beijing and had spent some years out of the country, he would have had to cultivate a whole new *guanxi* network. Research on overseas returnees (Du et al., 2021; Xiao & Wang, 2022) shows that while they may have developed greater resilience and entrepreneurial skills than their domestic counterparts, they will often struggle to secure the kinds of high-paying jobs they think they deserve due to unfamiliarity with China's labour market (which changes very fast) and limited opportunities to develop *guanxi*. In contrast, domestic graduates, while not possessing international capital, nevertheless possess more developed *guanxi* (networks and connections), which can help them to break into the labour market.

It was at this point, after a number of failures, that Ru decided to work in an international school: 'I just came back to Beijing, because I'm a local, and I went to an international school. I just want to change a little bit. I'm a programming guy. I'm an IT engineer'. Returning to Beijing would have made it easier for Ru to get back on his feet as he could rely on a local *guanxi* network – family and friends – to support him. While his turn to teaching appeared to be based on love rather than expediency, his first foray into international school teaching in 2015–2016 did not meet his expectations and ended in failure:

> I really love teaching, actually. But I didn't know at that moment. I just feel that they are lovely kids, but they did not listen to me. They [the original school] have a lot of bad students. They have a lot of emotions, feelings. They actually attacked my finger. So once, they closed the door very heavily. So they don't listen to my class. They just play their everything in the classroom and they don't listen to me. This was not a very good experience.

Although it was not clear why Ru chose this school (given the behavioural issues of the students), it might be surmised that he was unfamiliar with the international school market in Beijing or lacked the necessary teaching experience and qualifications to work in a more prestigious school. Despite lacking experience and professional accreditation, Ru's international capital was sufficient to secure him employment, even if the school itself appeared not to be that good. Ru, however, was undeterred by this negative experience. Interestingly, even though the students were disruptive, and even physically attacked him, he still described the students as 'lovely kids'. His empathy for the students might be attributed to his Christian faith which, as will be seen, became a source of strength on which he could draw to negotiate his time 'in the seaweed' of precarity.

Perhaps due to his bad experience, Ru next moved back into an IT-related position, although he would eventually circle back to international schooling a few years later:

> After that there is a very good job from Huawei. It gave me a lot of money. It was a very very high position. Then I went there. I changed my career again to IT. So I worked at Huawei last year, 2019. Corona virus comes here, and also we have US competition. Then I start to think: 'What is my goal? What is my dream?' So I realised that – actually I have some religious background. So I believe in Christianity, so I will see what is my calling. I pray a lot, and that is also helping. During the epidemic, Alibaba invited me to go there many times, but I didn't want to go. My passion is teaching, I think I must be a teacher no matter the salary.

Huawei designs, develops, manufactures, and sells telecommunications equipment, consumer electronics, smart devices, and various rooftop solar power products, while Alibaba is a Chinese multinational technology company specialising in e-commerce, retail, and technology. Both companies would have offered very attractive salaries and benefits, but as the so-called 996 companies (requiring workers to work from 9 am to 9 pm, six days a week), such benefits would have come at a high cost. Ru instead eschewed the more conventional pathway to success and, despite his previous negative experience, returned to international school teaching. Turning down a job from Alibaba would be considered an unwise move by many. As Ru put it, '[A] lot of my classmates and friends think I am crazy. From IT, that high salary, to teacher. I'm crazy. Logically, I'm crazy. But I just feel that'.

Ru's decision to exit the rat race could be understood as 'tang ping' or 'lying flat', a movement in China that has seen younger Chinese rejecting societal pressure to overwork and instead finding meaning in more attainable achievements, such as living on very little money or taking time to rest and rejuvenate. Ru's decision to reject the rat race may also be attributed to his faith, which helped him to discover what it was he was really striving for. Teaching ultimately emerged as a calling or a vocation. This was clarified in other parts of Ru's interview, where he reflected on the material advantages of working in IT, but which left him feeling emotionally bereft:

> So the emotion is, 'Go, go go!' I programme and I finish it. I earn a lot of money. But this one [teaching] lets me help others. It's totally different. Totally, totally different feeling. It's like I just feel happy. Simply, I feel happy.

In terms of motivation, Ru came to view extrinsic factors (such as salary and status) as hollow and meaningless and longed for something more profound, suggesting an altruistic orientation to teaching.

Significantly, the majority of the participants interviewed for this book did not view teaching in similarly altruistic terms as Ru. Rather, they were externally motivated, often becoming international school teachers in order to access the benefits offered by the sector (such as pay and access to a high-quality education for their children) or simply out of happenstance, rather than a clearly thought-out desire to be educators. For example, Jin (SD – chemistry teacher) reflected that working in an international school '[w]as a coincidence'. Gang (SD – physics teacher) stated that 'I think it's a coincidence that I entered an international school. Because, I am not actually a teacher training major, but I also came back from studying abroad'. Finally, Zuo yi (SD) explained that '[w]hen I was planning my career, I didn't want to be an international teacher. I was an international teacher because of some coincidence as well. I suddenly came into contact with this opportunity'.

The call of the international school dream: '[E]verything has worked out'

Although international school teaching was now Ru's calling, he did not return to international school teaching immediately but initially worked in a training centre – New Oriental – teaching mathematics. New Oriental is a provider of educational services in China, including language training, overseas and domestic test preparation courses, educational content and software, as well as online education. While the experience was not that inspiring or satisfying for Ru, it nevertheless provided him with the necessary teaching experience to level up and get a position in an international school:

> After all, I chose to go to education. The first is to go to New Oriental. I didn't have the chance to go there at the beginning, so in February 2020, I went to New Oriental to teach computer science. Also, I'm interested in computer science. They wanted me to teach maths, but I didn't want to, so I only taught computer science. But they didn't have a lot of students. So my department is VIP in America, so it is only teaching AP [Advanced Placement] class. And there were not a lot of students going to the US at that moment, especially because of the Corona virus. So I didn't have a lot of students. And I didn't feel that I was a teacher. I just worked there for two hours a week.

This dissatisfaction with working in the private school industry (which functioned as an entry point or gateway into international school teaching for some of the participants) was echoed by other participants – for example Rong (SCIS), Fen Fang (SCIS), and Shu (CCIS). Rong, for example, found the work to be tedious and repetitive:

> In New Oriental, we taught a lot of students at the same time, and you always taught the same subject. I normally taught IELTS writing and

reading, which means I taught more than 44,000 hours in the same subject in these three years. It's exhausting in the summer and winter, so I thought it's time to leave that place and get a new start.

Despite the negative experience, private training centres still provided the participants with the opportunity to acquire teaching experience or to put into perspective what they wanted to get out of their teaching careers. Ru's experience, for example, inspired him to look for a 'real' school, which would end up being NCIS in Beijing:

> Then I started to find some real school. New Oriental was a training school. I don't want a training school. Also, it was taking Sunday. So I went to apply, and NCIS is actually the only school. I found other schools, but they didn't give me an interview. So this is the only school that gave me an interview, and everything was very smooth. And I really like this school. You know, it's close to my home. And I found the students are really good. So it's really good. Everything has worked out.

The reference to 'it was taking Sunday' refers to Ru's Christian faith, with Sunday being an important day for him to worship. Ru's circuitous route into international schooling was also echoed by two other Returners, both of whom started out in careers other than teaching or education. Zixin (SCIS), who taught economics in SCIS, spent some time living and working in the United States and had a number of careers before finally ending up working in an international school:

> I went back to China in 2010, and my first job was in an investment company, but after that I started to teach English in a university in my home town. I'd been teaching English in the US for about three years. A friend told me that there was a chance and if I'm interested I could come to our international high school to teach economics. I said my job is basically about business administration, but he said I could get to know this subject and see if I was interested, so I started to teach economics by learning by doing, and now I've been teaching economics for eight years.

Similarly, Chang (SCIS), who taught Chinese in SCIS, also had a circuitous route into international schooling:

> Actually, I didn't study teaching when I was a college student. But after graduation, I worked in a Confucius Institute in Myanmar for three years as a Chinese teacher. During that time, I found that I was really interested in teaching Chinese, so after that I went to Hong Kong and got a master degree in Chinese, after which I chose to teach Chinese in mainland China.

While Chang spent time in Myanmar (an Asian country), the experience is nevertheless international in nature. Moreover, in the context of Mainland China, getting a master's degree from Hong Kong is synonymous with an overseas qualification and therefore enhanced Chang's international capital, which he was able to leverage to get a job in an international school on his return to Mainland China.

Reachers

Reachers are internal migrants who choose to 'decouple' (Yemini & Maxwell, 2018) from home because of structural barriers and utilise international school teaching to foster social mobility. As with Ru, before exploring Shu and Jin's journeys into international schooling, I first provide background information about the teaching profession in China as it informs many of Shu's experiences.

The teaching profession in China

The teaching force of China consists of about 17 million educators and administrators at various levels of the education system. Some 15 million teachers work in schools and kindergartens, teaching some 230 million students (Lo, 2019). Most Chinese teachers work in public schools that are controlled by the state. As such, all teaching-related aspects – such as credentials, recruitment, hiring, and registration – are provided, executed, or sanctioned by the state (Lo, 2019). Of the 15 million teachers, it is not clear how many work in private internationalised schools, although it is likely to be a small percentage of the overall teaching workforce.

Although teachers' social status in China is considered to be relatively high, their salaries remain incommensurate with their status (Lo, 2019). According to the Economic Research Institute (ERI, 2023), primary school teachers can earn between 131,646 yuan and 223,853 yuan a year, which equates to about 10,000 to 15,400 yuan a month. A public school teacher's salary is likely to increase over time, as teachers become more experienced and gain more qualifications. The emergence of new and well-paying occupations since the 1990s, such as information technology, finance, and communication, has further eroded the attractiveness of teaching, with competitive high-school students tending to avoid choosing teaching as an academic major at university (Lo, 2019).

Despite its low salary, public school teaching in China is still considered an attractive career for some due to its relatively stable nature, which is captured in the metaphor of the 'iron rice bowl'. Although teachers in public schools are not officially considered civil servants in China, they are contracted by the government under the *bian zhi* system (Liang et al., 2016).

According to Liang et al. (2016, p. 71), *bian zhi* is similar to the concept of lifelong tenure:

> A teacher has to pass a specific exam and obtain approval from the district Department of Education to be granted a *bian zhi*. Teachers with a *bian zhi* are entitled to medical benefits, a housing stipend, and pensions, while temporary or substitute teachers do not have such privileges.

However, cities such as Shanghai and Beijing have recently ended the lifelong tenure of teachers. For example, all public teachers in Shanghai now have to renew their teacher certification and be evaluated once every five years and can only obtain tenure (*bian zhi*) after five consecutive renewals (Liang et al., 2016). Despite this, public school teaching is relatively secure, particularly when compared to international school teaching, where teachers continue to be employed on short-term contracts (often two years) that need to be continually renegotiated to guarantee continued employment (Bunnell, 2016)

There are two main pathways to becoming a teacher in China. The first, and the most common, is for teachers to attend a Normal university. The term 'Normal' is derived from the French *normale* – for example, Ecole Normale – and refers to the aspiration of educational institutions to cultivate certain norms among students. Examples of famous Normal universities in China include East China Normal University (in Shanghai) and Beijing Normal University. Normal universities train students to become teachers, but more recently they have also started to cultivate a more comprehensive curriculum (Lo, 2019). While Normal universities offer a range of courses, including, education, academic subjects, and political education, they give relatively little attention to the practice of teaching (Lo, 2019). Perhaps because of this, since 2017, graduates from Normal universities must sit and pass the National Teacher Certificate Examination (Lee, 2019). The second route into teaching is to complete an undergraduate degree and then sit and pass the National Teacher Certificate Examination. Lo (2019) and Li et al. (2019) offer a more detailed overview of public school teaching in China.

In contrast to the public school sector, the private (*minban*) international school sector is less regulated by the state, although, as Chapter 2 made clear, this has started to change with the introduction of greater regulations since 2021. For example, teachers are not required to pass the National Teacher Certificate Examination. Moreover, due to their for-profit, private nature, internationalised schools are in a position to offer better salaries to host country national teachers than would be available in public schools (Hammer, 2021). At the same time, there still remains a large 'ethnic gap' (Hammer, 2021) between foreign teachers' and host country national teachers' salaries (Hammer, 2021; Hatch, 2020; Machin, 2021). Therefore, while host country national teachers are economically privileged when compared to teachers in public schools, they are relatively disadvantaged when compared to expatriate teachers in international schools, who still receive the highest salaries and greatest benefits. Despite this, it has been argued that host country national teachers may still be satisfied with working in international schools, due to the perceived, relatively better work environment and conditions than in equivalent schools in the national system (Canterford, 2003).

Shu's journey (or 'this school provides me with a shelter')

When I interviewed Shu in early 2020, she was in her early thirties and had been working as a language assistant in a prestigious international school (CCIS) in Shanghai that modelled itself on the private British boarding school model. After struggling to find a place as a public school teacher and working for a number of private training companies, Shu finally found some security and stability at CCIS. Significantly, Shu had been working at CCIS for seven years. Given that most teachers in international schools tend to remain in a school for the short term (perhaps two to three years), Shu might also be thought of as a Remainer teacher.

Understanding Shu's frustrated experiences of becoming a public school teacher further complexifies the host country national teacher experience. It shows that teachers do not always 'simply' transition from public schooling to private international schooling (Rey et al., 2020), but they often struggle to find a place in the public education system due to inequality and discrimination, which forms the catalyst for seeking alternative careers in international schools.

'I want to be an English teacher: I want to teach'

Unlike many of the other participants who fell into teaching through happenstance or coincidence, Shu always knew that she wanted to be a teacher from a young age:

> When I was in middle school, I wanted to be a teacher. I don't know. I just felt like this was an instinct. This idea just came to me very very clearly: I want to be a Chinese teacher. I want to teach. I think I can teach well.

Like many of the participants, however, her route into international school teaching would not be straightforward. Shu's decision to attend a Normal university was not just based on her dream to become a teacher but also based on her family's precarious socio-economic situation:

> Because my family was not really rich, and they could not support me very well, we made a decision for me to go to a Normal institute, which is a teacher's college. My plan was to go into the Chinese department to

learn Chinese. At that time, most students would choose science because the schools were mostly open to science majors. My dream was to study Chinese, to learn literature.

Given their financial situation, Shu's parents may have considered public school teaching to offer the most secure route into employment upon graduation. As mentioned earlier, public school teaching in China lags behind other industries in terms of pay, but it does provide an 'iron rice bowl', which guarantees a certain amount of stability and security.

However, Shu's plan did not go according to plan, as the university unexpectedly 'didn't take' her. Consequently, Shu decided to change subjects: 'A compromise was I ended up in the English department'. It was not clear from the interview why the university did not accept Shu to study Chinese. As Chinese is a very competitive subject at university (with English being less so), it might be surmised that Shu may have lost out to other students due to intense competition or she may have not met the entry requirements to study Chinese. Despite this set back, changing subjects and studying English, which presumably had lower entrance requirements, allowed Shu to get back on track and pursue her goal of becoming a public school teacher, even if it was not the subject she had dreamt about as a middle-school student.

Once she had graduated, Shu started to look for a position as a public school English teacher. However, the process was far more complicated and competitive than she had anticipated:

> I didn't stay in my home city for long because if you want to work in a public school you need to pass government examinations. Oral test, written test, and after that there was an interview. So, I passed the oral and the written test, but the interview session, the competition was even fiercer, and there was a little bit of dodgy play over there. There were very few vacancies, but so many graduates. So, people were trying very very hard to get a position. The teachers in the public school are 'within the system' (*bian zhi*) So they are basically treated similarly as civil servants. It's a job for life. So, everybody wants to get that. But again, I failed that. I failed that.

As mentioned earlier, public school teaching may not offer competitive salaries, but it does offer stability. As Shu mentioned, teachers in public schools are considered to be civil servants; therefore, despite low salaries, they enjoy employment security. The phrase 'little bit of dodgy play' suggests that the selection process may have been open to corruption, with some candidates perhaps leveraging their *guanxi* (i.e. connections or social capital) as a way to cut corners and jump to the front of the candidate queue. This implicates social class as a salient factor mediating teachers' journey into international school teaching, as those with greater social and cultural capital are in a position to cultivate greater *guanxi*/social capital, which they can leverage to get ahead in the rat race. As Shu's family were 'not rich', she could not cultivate nor deploy *guanxi* networks and therefore had to rely solely on meritocracy, which left her less competitive than her better-connected peers.

As a consequence, Shu decided to 'decouple' (Yemini & Maxwell, 2018) from home and search for positions further afield. By becoming mobile (i.e. becoming an internal migrant), Shu was able to maximise her chances of securing a position as a public school teacher. However, once again, she encountered difficulty, this time in the form of discrimination due to her new status as a *wai di* teacher: 'Public school was out of bounds for non-local people. They don't welcome *wai di* teachers'. The term *wai di* is a colloquial expression which roughly translates as 'outsider'. In theory, public schools can employ teachers from any city in China. However, as suggested by Shu, in practice they often discriminate in favour of teachers who possess a *hukou* of the city where the school is located. While schools are in a position to offer some *wai di* teachers a *hukou*, the quota is limited, and schools will only do so for the most outstanding candidates. As will become evident, securing a *hukou* is essential for teachers, as it determines access to education and healthcare, something which becomes more significant for teachers once they settle down, marry, have children, and become Remainers.

The *hukou* household registration system was created in the 1950s and was used to assign citizens to agricultural (rural) and non-agricultural (urban) status (Hao et al., 2014). Workers' employment and social benefits, such as healthcare, social security, and education, are inextricably tied to their *hukou* registration (Wu & Wallace, 2021). Since the 1950s, the *hukou* system has evolved to allow greater mobility between rural and urban areas, which has seen massive rural-to-urban migration of people to China's larger cities, such as Beijing, Shanghai, and Guangzhou (Wu & Wallace, 2021). The *hukou* system has further been modified to allow for the conversion of *hukou*, thereby allowing certain *rencai* (talents) who meet nationally and locally determined criteria to transfer their *hukou* status from their birthplace to a new urban area (Wu & Wallace, 2021).

Despite these changes, the *hukou* system is still associated with educational stratification (Hao et al., 2014) and remains a 'key pillar of Chinese inequality' (Wu & Wallace, 2021, p. 224), which has evolved into a 'powerful institution of the socialist state for controlling the population' (Wu & Wallace, 2021, p. 224). Attaining a new *hukou* requires an individual to own property or to have the funds to be able to cut corners and purchase one semi-legally through *guanxi* networks (He, 2011). Moreover, many individuals from rural areas are blocked from attaining urban *hukou* status due to not being able to meet the requirements, thereby resulting in millions of workers remaining tied to their birthplace, resulting in limited opportunities for advancement (Wu & Wallace, 2021).

Teachers like Shu, who come from economically disadvantaged backgrounds and who wish to work in affluent cities like Shanghai and Beijing, are effectively locked out of the public school system due to structural inequalities created by corruption, a lack of *guanxi*, and issues associated with the *hukou* system. This was echoed by Li (SD), who was similarly unable to work in a public school in the city she had moved to due to *hukou* complications:

> Because my *hukou* was not registered in Jiangsu, I did not directly apply to be a public school teacher. Public school positions in Jiangsu Province are preferred for those with a Jiangsu household registration, so opportunities for people from other provinces, like me, are relatively limited.

'Training institutions were still hot'

Seeing her dream of becoming a teacher disintegrate before her eyes, Shu considered studying for a postgraduate qualification. This is a strategy that is increasingly being adopted by younger Chinese who wish to become more competitive, as well as delay their entry into an oversaturated marketplace (Tai, 2017). However, Shu was not able to pursue this option as, in her words, 'my family didn't allow me to do that'. The reason for not allowing Shu to study was not explicitly stated but may be related to the family's financial situation, as well as Shu's gender. For example, Yao's (2022) study of gender differences in post-college plans of China's college students found that family socio-economic resources and anticipated parenthood timing are associated with post-college plans, with these associations being more pronounced among women.

Shu may have been locked out of the public school sector, but her teaching qualifications helped her to secure a position in the private tutoring industry:

> It was a private institute for adults to learn English. I taught them basic grammar knowledge. It was the first job of my life. I was able to learn many things, to meet with people. But I didn't improve my teaching that much because you just explored what your customer needs. It was mostly one-on-one teaching, and I felt like it was just tutoring. But teaching in a school was still something I wanted to do.

Shu was not the only participant to start their teaching career in the private tutoring industry. Jin, for example, also started his teaching career in private tutoring, which at the time was a lucrative and relatively stable industry:

> In 2011, I graduated from college, and at that time, according to the level of our school, I could go back home to a high school or junior school in the county. But I was unwilling, so I wanted to go out and make a break for myself. Then I went to Shenzhen. At that time, training institutions were

still hot in all aspects, so finding a job was very easy. I went to a training institution first, and I came into contact with international courses. My English was relatively good, so I took the international course.

Prior to 2020, the private tutoring industry was worth an estimated 7.5 billion US dollars (46.3 billion RMB), representing more than 50,000 international and domestically owned language centres (Fish et al., 2017). In 2020, the Chinese government introduced a series of policies – colloquially known as the 'Double Reduction Policy' (*Shuang Jian*) – designed to reduce the academic burden of students in the compulsory education stage. In addition to reducing students' homework, the Double Reduction Policy also regulated the private tutoring industry. Consequently, institutions offering disciplinary subjects such as history, physics, chemistry, mathematics, or foreign languages (such as English, Japanese, or Russian) were prevented from offering off-campus classes or tutoring services to students in compulsory education (Grades 1 to 9). Conversely, non-disciplinary subjects that focused on concerted cultivation, such as sports, music, and art, were not impacted by the new policy (Zhong, 2023).

The impact of these reforms has been devastating. Major players in the private tutoring industry, such as New Oriental, TAL Education Group, and Gaotu Techedu, have had to lay off many employees and re-brand themselves (offering non-disciplinary subjects), while smaller companies have gone bankrupt (Wu, 2021). A study of ten former private tutors by Yang et al. (2023) found that they struggled to find positions in public schools, perhaps due to a negative perception of the tutoring industry. Instead, they went into media-related careers and sales. Although participants like Shu and Jin left the private tutoring sector before the implementation of the Double Reduction Policy, it is not unreasonable to assume that many former tutors may seek refuge in the international school sector. International schools are more likely to value former private tutors' experiences as there is less stigma around the private, for-profit nature of the work, as international schools often operate in a similar fashion (although this has started to change in the wake of the regulation of the international school sector in China; see Chapter 2 for more on this).

'If you work more, you earn more'

Luckily for the participants in this study, their exit from the private tutoring industry came before its evisceration. However, the speed with which the industry was dismantled highlights its inherent precariousness, which Shu experienced after moving to Shanghai:

> Then I moved to Shanghai. The first job I had when I arrived in Shanghai was working in a training centre. The business was okay. It was thriving in

the first two years and they opened several branches downtown in Shanghai, like Xu Jia Hui and Pu Dong and Jing An Temple. But in the second year, because the investor stopped providing us with the money, the school went bankrupt. And we were not even told that. It was very very sad. The day I went to work and I was told, 'You've lost your job. They owe you one month's salary'. So that gave me a very strong sense of insecurity.

As the cosmopolitan and economic heart of China, Shanghai is a popular destination for China's internal migrants and expatriates alike. Despite the lure of the city, Shu found herself in a precarious and unpredictable situation, where a school might thrive one year only to experience a sudden downturn the next due to financial crises or aggressive government intervention. The sudden demise of the private tutoring industry in China is testament to this inherent insecurity.

For Shu, working in the private tutoring sector was primarily a means to an end, simply providing her with a way to earn a living:

Then I worked in some training centres for children because the market was good. For adults, it was risky. It depends on the money invested in the business. But for the kid's market, teenager market, even though you don't need a lot of money, you can still run a very successful school because of its reputation. And because of the high volume of work, we worked from 8 until 10 pm. But we could have a break from 10 am to 3 pm. But after 4, when the kids finished school, after 4 until 10 was the teaching time. Our rush hour. I made some money at that time because every month the salary was okay to support me and I had a little bit of savings. That's one reason why the training schools attract people. They say, *duo lao duo de* – 'If you work more, you earn more'.

While she was able to earn a fairly good living, the frenetic pace and the unpredictable nature of the private tutoring industry left Shu feeling frustrated and tired. This was echoed by other participants, such as Rong (SCIS) recounted earlier. Despite the negativity associated with the private tutoring sector, it would nevertheless play a formative role in some of the participants' journeys into international school teaching, providing them with the necessary pedagogical and international capital to break into and find a place in the international school sector.

'This school provides me with a shelter, a box'

Having become dissatisfied with private tutoring, Shu sought a 'way out' by sending her CV to prospective schools, which also included international schools:

Every year, I would send my resume. Every year, seeking a way out of this programme because it was too tiring. I feel like I was exhausted at that

Arrival 63

time. I sent out lots of resumes to schools and this one [CCIS] replied. I had been working in training centres for six years, both teaching adults and tutoring teenagers. And then seven years ago I joined CCIS and found that this is the place I really wanted to be. It's a school, it's not people running a business. The school has a mission, vision, and they have a clear goal. But before that, the goal of training centres was just to make money.

Shu's decision to work in an international school was not the result of coincidence but necessity, as a way to escape the private tutoring industry. Even though her position at CCIS did not allow Shu to realise her dream to be a teacher as such, it nevertheless provided her with benefits and opportunities:

I was hired by CCIS as a Teaching Assistant. To be honest, when it comes to language support, I feel like I'm teaching Dummy's English. I know that academic English sounds really really fancy, but it is not academic at all.

Working in an international school is akin to 'reaching' as it represents a significant form of social mobility that confers higher status than working as a tutor. Being a private tutor provides the necessary experience, resilience, and training for some teachers to become more socially mobile and hoist themselves up from out of precarity to relative stability.

I now return to the experiences of Jin (SD), who can also be said to be a Reacher. Like Shu (NCIS), Jin was able to leverage his experience working in the private tutoring sector to jump to international school teaching:

Then after two years of work [in the private tutoring sector], I had the opportunity to work in an international school, so I entered the industry and worked in that school for a year. After that, I went to a school in Beijing, because my home town is Henan, and it is closer to my home town, so I came to Beijing.

However, Jin represents a different kind of Reacher. Whereas Shu was (at the time of her interview) single and without children, Jin was married and had two children. His decision to move to Beijing was motivated by a desire to be closer to his home town, therefore suggesting that he also shares some features of Remainer teachers (to be discussed later). However, once in Beijing, Jin found that it was difficult for him and his family to settle in the city due to complications with the *hukou* system, which made accessing schools for his children difficult:

Because I have two children now. In Beijing, I can't solve the problem of Beijing household registration. At the beginning, that school promised me to solve my registration, but after seven years of working there, it still didn't help me. With two children in Beijing, I will be in great trouble in the future. If I have only one child, I can send him to an international school, there is no problem, but with two children, it may be a bit difficult. After all, if I come here [SD], it is not difficult to solve the problem of household registration. So based on this situation, I made a new choice.

Enrolling a child in a public school in Beijing, as in many big cities in China, is a complex and largely inequitable process, with priority being given to individuals who own property and/or hold a Beijing *hukou*. The verb 'solve' gives a sense of how inherently problematic the *hukou* system is for many Chinese citizens. As a *wai di* teacher, Jin did not possess a Beijing *hukou* and therefore struggled to find a public school for his children. His precarious situation was also exacerbated by the size of his family, perhaps an unintended social consequence of the abolition of the one-child policy, which ostensibly sought to address the social and demographic damage wrought by China's one-child policy, which was implemented from 1980 to 2016, but which, as noted, also appears to have created new struggles that Chinese families must negotiate on their own. Jin may have been able to find a way around the *hukou* situation if he had just one child as he may have been able to send them to the international school he worked at in Beijing. This is a strategy employed by Remainer teachers, such as Ying. However, sending two children to an international school may have been too expensive, as the school may have only offered one tuition waiver or his salary would not have been sufficient to cover the costs of privately educating two children. Jin thus decided to leave Beijing and move to a smaller, though still significant, city, where it was easier to 'solve' the *hukou* problem.

Returning to Shu, working in an international school provided her with the stability she had lacked in her previous positions as a private tutor which enabled her to plan for the future:

> This school provides me with a shelter, a box, food, housing for my five cats. And it's safe in this box. If I go outside, I don't know whether the school will provide me with similar things. The salary is okay, but it is okay for me. I can save some money. I can save for my future, pension and all that kind of stuff. But I know this is not the perfect place to stay.

The shelter may not be overly grand – she likens it to a box (i.e. it is functional and utilitarian) – but it nevertheless provided her with what she had been desperately seeking since graduating – relative security. Significantly, even though Shu had managed to reach some stability, she was still aware that international school teaching entailed its own type of precarity:

> And also, in Shanghai within the whole system, there are public schools and private-schools, so they also follow Gao Kao. But for private school, they don't need a restriction on *hukou*. So, teachers can work there with a

Arrival 65

higher salary, with the same social benefit, but you don't have this long-term stability. They can sack you. They can end the contract.

As mentioned earlier, international school teaching has been characterised as inherently precarious because of its short-term nature, due to the practice of hiring faculty on short-term contracts (Bunnell, 2016; Poole, 2019; Poole & Bunnell, 2021). Significantly, Shu was not the only participant who was conscious of the precarity that went hand in hand with international school teaching. For example, Jing (SCIS) observed that 'in China, private-schools are not as stable as public schools'. For Reacher teachers like Shu, the shadow of precarity is never far away. While international schools provide them with some stability, that stability is tenuous at best. As Shu notes, a school can end a contract whenever they choose. In contrast to public school teaching, where the teacher is akin to a civil servant and therefore can expect to have a job for life, private international schools are more precarious. The examples above suggest that not only is precarity experienced by both expatriate and host country national teachers – lending credence to the argument that precarity is a structural feature of international school teaching (Poole & Bunnell, 2021) – but the kinds of precarity experienced by host country national teachers may be qualitatively different from those experienced by expatriate teachers.

Despite the precarity, the benefits of working in an international school appeared to outweigh the potential difficulties. Socially mobile teachers like Shu and Jin might thus be said to be in a position of 'precarious privilege' (Rey et al., 2020), as the economic advantages of working in international schools comes at the cost of being precariously employed.

Remainers

Remainers are usually married and have children. As such, they choose to be 'closely coupled to home' (Yemini & Maxwell, 2018) and are motivated to work in international schools due to convenience as well as the educational advantage doing so offers their children. As with the previous sections, I begin by considering key concepts for understanding Remainers. The first is recent reconceptualisations of immobility, which I employ to nuance Remainers' decision to stay in place as a form of strategic 'spatial continuity' (Schewel, 2020). The second is the notion of the *xiaokang* and '*xiaokang* parents' which I use to position Remainers as aspiring, yet precariously positioned, members of China's expanding middle class, who are able to participate in school choice by working in international schools.

Immobility

The international school teacher is often represented as an intrepid globetrotting adventurer moving from country to country in search of new experiences.

Prior research into international school teacher mobility (Bailey, 2015; Poole & Bunnell, 2023) reinforces this representation, with mobility generally being seen as a positive feature of international schooling and the preserve of the expatriate teacher. In contrast, teachers who are less mobile or immobile, such as host country national teachers, have received less attention. The reason for this neglect may be due to the mobility construct itself, which positions mobility as inherently positive and worthy of study. In contrast, immobility carries with it negative connotations, with being immobile equalling being stuck in place (Ravn, 2022). The so-called Stayers (Ravn, 2022) are depicted as 'failures' (Looker & Naylor, 2009) or as disempowered subjects who are 'left behind' against their will (Forsberg, 2019). This has been referred to as a mobility bias (Schewel, 2020). As alluded to above, the same bias is evident in the international school literature, as typified by Hardman (2001), who labelled teachers who had remained in one school for many years as Penelopes, effectively having outstayed their usefulness and perhaps being unaware of it.

However, mobility scholars have begun to move 'beyond the binary of mobility as a positive experience and immobility as a negative development' (Chou, 2021, p. 750) in order to view immobility more positively (e.g. Coleman, 2022; Ravn, 2022; Schewel, 2020). For example, Coleman's (2022) monograph, *Class, place, and higher education: Experiences of homely mobility* reconsidered the seemingly negative notion of immobility from the perspective of lived experience. Rather than fixating on working-class students' 'passive withdrawal from the world' (p. 39), Coleman instead proposed that studying close to home can foster both agency and self-expansion. Therefore, when considering the experiences of those who are less mobile or immobile (such as some host country national teachers), it is necessary to move beyond the mobility/immobility dichotomy to consider the subjective intentions that lay behind decisions to stay or go. Immobility, therefore, is not just imposed (though this may indeed the case) and structural, but it can also be elected (Bailey, 2021, with individuals choosing to remain immobile in order to further their own agendas.

As part of this attempt to reconceptualise immobility, scholars have sought to develop a more positive scholarly vocabulary to describe. One such term which informs much of my subsequent analysis is that of 'spatial continuity' (Schewel, 2020). Spatial continuity is defined as an individual's 'centre of gravity over a period of time' (Schewel, 2020, p. 329) and recognises that 'immobility is never absolute, as indeed all people move in their everyday lives – to school, to work, to the market' (Schewel, 2020, p. 329). Far from being disempowered or left behind, immobility becomes a strategy for individuals to negotiate precarity and to foster greater agency and stability. Thus, immobility may be characterised by 'continuity in one's centre of gravity, or place of residence, relative to spatial and temporal frames' (Schewel, 2020, p. 329).

The notion of immobility as a positive and nuanced concept helps me to understand host country national teachers' decision to remain 'closely coupled to home' (Yemini & Maxwell, 2018) more empathetically. This is necessary because the notion of mobility and constant movement has been baked into the construct of the international school teacher. As prior research shows (e.g. Bailey, 2015; Bright, 2022; Rey et al., 2020), expatriate teachers value mobility highly, and often choose to work in international schools because it facilitates constant movement. However, the same expectation cannot be applied to Remainers, as their cultural and personal circumstances differ considerably from those of expatriate teachers. In order to understand Remainers more positively and on their own terms I next turn to the notion of '*xiaokang* parents'.

Xiaokang *parents*

The term '*xiaokang* parent' refers to a social group who have reached a situation of relative stability – they own a house, a car, do not have debt, and are able to invest in their child(ren)'s educational futures (Cutri, 2022). They occupy a somewhat ambiguous position in China's wealthy social hierarchy, which also includes the *guan er dai* (children of government officials) and the *fu er dai* (a new wealthy entrepreneurial class) (Cutri, 2022). The *guan er dai* possess *guanxi*, while the *fu er dai* possess economic capital, but lack political *guanxi*. The notion of the *xiaokang* aligns with the second, entrepreneurial group. While *xiaokang* parents favour key point (*zhong dian*) public schools – as they offer a pathway to elite domestic universities, such as Peking or Fudan – entrance into such schools is both selective and difficult (Cutri, 2022). Rather than risk sending their child to a *pu tong* (e.g. ordinary) school, where they may underperform and therefore score poorly on the university entrance examination (Gao Kao), *xiaokang* parents may instead opt to send their child to an international school (Cutri, 2022; Young, 2018).

Significantly, the teachers in this study (particularly Remainers) were neither *guan er dai*, *fu er dai* nor completely *xiaokang*. They may have achieved relative stability (possessing property, perhaps through intergenerational wealth) but they did not possess the economic capital or political *guanxi* to engage in school choice for their children (i.e. overcoming *hukou* issues or paying high tuition fees so their children could study in private international schools). However, they did possess the international capital to work in international schools, through which they were able to engage in school choice. Remainers, therefore, represent a precariously aspirational *xiaokang*, who are pragmatically driven to move from precarity to stability by deploying their international capital to gain employment in international schools as a way to access educational advantage for their children that otherwise would remain inaccessible.

It also has to be noted that the *xiaokang* concept has applicability not just to Remainer teachers but also to Reachers and Returners. In fact, both Ying and Gang straddle multiple categories of teacher. For example, Ying, as will be shown, may be a Remainer, but she used her immobility in an aspirational

68 *Arrival*

sense, and therefore might also be thought of as a Reacher. Similarly, Gang embodied aspects of Returners, Reachers, and Reaminers. However, I consider him to be a Remainer as his interviews suggested that being 'closely coupled to home' (Yemini & Maxwell, 2018) was a long-term motivation of his, even if it required making detours in the form of strategic 'jumps' to other schools to realise it.

Ying's journey: '[F]amily reasons may be more important'

Ying had been working at SD for about seven years when interviewed in 2022. Like many of the participants in this book, she did not start out as an international school teacher; rather, she began her career in tertiary education:

> In fact, I have been in the international field for a long time, more than ten years, but my field started from eleven or twelve years ago. I taught Chinese as a foreign language in a university. I taught students in the international college of the university. The students came from Japan, South Korea, Singapore, Germany, and the United States. In the university, the international college actually had many undergraduates and exchange students, as well as social personnel.

After giving birth to her first child, Ying decided to leave and work at SD:

> For me, family reasons may be more important. I happened to have a baby at the time, and my two children study here now. Well, yes, so there may be many mothers with the same reasons. I saw that some of our colleagues would change jobs and come to our school. Most of the time, they brought their children just to study in the first grade, and transferred from another school. So maybe for mum, I think the educational resources of children may be a very important consideration. I might think about what kind of different education I can provide for my children.

Like many countries, educational resources in China are unequally distributed, but education remains in practice the only pathway to secure a successful and stable future. This educational imperative is not just a recent phenomenon but can be traced back to China's Imperial Examination, a civil service examination system in Imperial China administered for the purpose of selecting candidates for the state bureaucracy. Its legacy lives on in the university entrance Gao Kao examination. The popular saying, *wan ban jie xia pin, wei you du shu gao* (learning is above everything else) captures the importance of education as the safest way to realise social mobility. While alternative forms of education have started to develop (such as vocational education), they remain under-resourced and are perceived by *xiaokang* parents as inferior to university-based pathways (Zeng, 2021), which are imbued with greater symbolic and cultural capital.

Connected to the above are the rising costs of bringing up a child (or increasingly, children) and paying for their education. As mentioned earlier, the Double Reduction Policy has been introduced, in part, to alleviate the financial burden placed on parents and to encourage them to have more babies to address China's declining birth rate and ageing population. Faced with limited and precarious pathways to normative success, *xiaokang* parents like Ying deploy a strategy of 'spatial continuity' (Schewel, 2020) in order to leverage intergenerational familial capital – that is economic, symbolic, and *guanxi* capital. For Ying, working in an international school thus became a 'counter-strategy' (Forsberg, 2019) for escaping precarity while also remaining aspirational:

> There is another reason [for joining SD], actually, for me personally, because I happen to live near this school. This is why I have never left my job in this school because you will have a lot of comprehensive considerations.

I use the term counter-strategy to describe Ying's motivation to remain 'closely coupled to home' (Yemini & Maxwell, 2018), as mobility is often considered to be a marker of privilege and typically takes the positive pole in the mobility–immobility dichotomy. However, in China, internal migration is a loose assemblage of precarious and aspirational realities. Internal migration is often associated with rural-based citizens, who will move hundreds of miles from their families to take up construction or factory-based employment in urban centres to make more money. At the same time, there is a sizeable white-collar internal migrant workforce, which encompasses teachers like Shu and Jin, who are compelled to be mobile in order to overcome structural barriers created by the *hukou* system. While parents like Ying lack the economic capital of their *xiaokang* counterparts, they are nevertheless able to engage in strategic immobility from a relatively privileged position. For example, Ying was able to work in an international school in part because of her international capital (which she accrued through her prior higher education experience). She was also able to work in an international school because it was located near her. At the same time, Ying's ability to be mobile was circumscribed by her familial situation – she was married and had children. Therefore, even if she had wanted to be mobile, she may have not been able to; yet within this immobility, she was able to exercise some agency by engaging in school choice for her children.

Ying was not the only female participant to send her child to the school they worked at. Mei (SCIS), for example, started her career as a public school teacher, 'quit teaching' for ten years, and then returned to the profession to work at SCIS. Her decision to return to teaching may have been based on her daughters' age – 'I got back to teaching when she started junior high'.

Although her interview did not explicitly explain why she wanted her daughter to study at SCIS, it could be concluded that having spent some time overseas, Mei may have seen the value of an international education for her daughter, perhaps even considering sending her abroad at a later date or wishing to spare her the trauma of competing in the high-stakes Gao Kao examination.

Ying also considered proximity to family to be an important consideration: 'My family lives nearby, and children can study here, and then I can work here with peace of mind. So actually family and children are a more important criteria for me'. Extrinsic factors, such as proximity to family and convenience, were also a significant motivator for other participants. For example, Lu Wen (SCIS) was motivated to work in SCIS because it allowed her to continue her previous job and remain close to her family:

> This kind of job is similar to what I did before, and SCIS is very close to my family in Town X. So I wanted to come back close to my family and do my old job. I never worked in a school before. I was in a counsellor company, so I just wanted to give it a go.

Lu Wen's use of 'just' gives a sense of being untroubled about her career change, which contrasts with Ying's more strategic reasons for working in an international school. Lu Wen also viewed working in an international school as a means to an end, so she could remain close to her family and continue her 'old job' as a school counsellor.

Similarly, Rong was motivated to work at SCIS due to its convenience, which also underscores the salience of extrinsic factors for host country national teachers: 'My home is in Town X, so SCIS is quite a short distance and I can drive from home. So I chose SCIS'.

Significantly, the verb 'chose' suggests a sense of agency. From Rong's perspective, she 'chose' to work at the school because it allowed her to drive to work. This reason may appear trivial, particularly when compared to the other participants' narratives. However, it needs to be interpreted within the context of a more positive interpretation of immobility and spatial continuity. A significant proportion of the participants were women and were married. Therefore, it can be assumed that issues related to property were already taken care of. Within the context of relative stability, many teachers may prioritise convenience and stability over mobility, which, while offering greater possibilities, nevertheless creates a certain amount of uncertainty. Or if they were not married, they may have lived with their parents or were able to depend financially on them. It is still common in China for the groom (and the groom's family) to provide the three 'haves': *you qian* (have money/savings), *you che* (have car), *you fang* (have property without mortgage), or at the very minimum possess *cai* (talent, e.g., be highly educated) to be able to provide the three 'haves' in the future.

In contrast to the previous two examples, Meng, who was a director of curriculum at SCIS, had more complex reasons for working at SCIS:

> I came here last year. The city's municipal government had called all international divisions of public schools to a stop. They banned all international divisions and asked them to transfer into private international schools. So teachers originally from there had to go into private-schools. I didn't want to get far from my home town, so SCIS became an appropriate destination. So it was because of family and policy.

Like the other participants, Meng wanted to remain close to his family. At the same time, his initial motivation for working at SCIS was triggered by the closure of the international division in the public school he formerly worked at. This closure might be interpreted as the local government's response to the regulation of the international school industry (see Chapter 2), as well as the impact of COVID-19, which saw fewer students choosing to study overseas, thereby impacting enrolment numbers. While he could have become mobile and moved (as both Gang and Jin did), he appeared to be committed to the locale as his family were there.

Overall, working in an international school for Remainer teachers is largely extrinsic in nature – that is a means to an end and largely focused on accruing material benefits to support family – with no evidence of intrinsic or altruistic motivations. Having explored Ying's reasons for working in an international school, I next consider the motivations and experiences of Gang. Juxtaposing Gang and Ying's narratives suggests a gendered response to precarity and becoming an aspirational *xiaokang* that current research has yet to consider.

Gang's journey: '[I]t's the school on our doorstep'

At the time of being interviewed in 2022, Gang had been working at SD for just three months. Prior to this, he had worked in an international school in his home town as a physics teacher for about six years:

> I think it's a coincidence that I entered an international school. Because, I am not actually a teacher training major, but I also came back from studying abroad. At that time, there was a famous school near our home, and then an international school opened in this famous school. Then I thought that my children would go to school and work closer later, so I planned to go to this international school department for a job interview. And then the recruitment process was relatively smooth to enter this school. There are also a few teachers I know, just because it's the school on our doorstep.

Similar to many of the participants, Gang did not plan to work in an international school, but fell into international school teaching through 'coincidence'. In his case, he returned from studying abroad and was able to find a job relatively easily because he was able to deploy the international capital accrued from his overseas study. In many respects Gang is a Returner; however, his formative overseas experiences appeared to be less significance to him than Ru's. While Gang did not offer details about why he wanted his children to study at the school, it can be inferred with reference to Ying's interview excerpts that doing so facilitated access to educational advantage for his children (i.e. an international curriculum) that would have been out of reach under normal circumstances. Once again, a strong extrinsic, pragmatic form of motivation can be discerned, which appears to be a response to precarity. As established earlier, contemporary China is highly precarious even for middle-class parents due to uncertain policies (e.g. Double Reduction Policy) and the absence of a social security net; therefore, stability and an aspirational *xiaokang* mindset may drive teachers' actions, which might help to explain why teachers like Ying and Gang elected to be immobile.

Initially, Gang considered working in the school to be relatively easy and remained there for six years:

> In fact, when I went in, I didn't encounter too many difficulties. After all, it's on the doorstep. And then I went, and then I tried it, and then I found that everything was okay. And then I have been working in this industry for six years.

However, just three months before being interviewed, Gang made the decision to leave his home town and move to SD. It was not clear from the interview the proximity of this city from his home town, but Gang's choice of the verb 'jump' suggests that, subjectively speaking, it was some distance:

> I jumped to this school from another school. I only came to this school for about three months. The main reason I came to this school is that I have seen all the conditions, and I think it's okay. The source of students, I think is also okay. And then it can also solve the problem of my children's education. And then the welfare benefits in all aspects are better. So I considered coming to this school to give it a try.

Ultimately, Gang's main reason for moving to the school appeared to be related to the benefits it offered, once again underscoring the significance of extrinsic factors for host country national teachers. While he was not explicit about the nature of these benefits – 'the welfare benefits in all aspects are better' – they were clearly superior to those offered by the 'school on our doorstep' as he was willing to risk 'jumping' to a new school.

Like Ying, Gang's reasons for 'decoupling' (Yemini & Maxwell, 2018) from the locale were also based on accruing educational advantage for his children. In this instance, moving from his home town to a new school helped him to 'solve the problem' of his children's education. Significantly, Gang, like some of the other participants, used the verb 'solve' when discussing issues related to the *hukou* system and children's education (with these two often being interconnected). This collocation suggests that *hukou* and education in China are inextricably linked to difficulties and struggle. Gang considered working in an international school to be the most effective strategy to get his children into a good school. As mentioned at the beginning of this chapter, *xiaokang* parents have a preference to send their children to 'key point' (*Zhong dian*) public schools. However, this may not be desirable or even possible for teachers like Gang, who as an aspirational *xiaokang*, lack the financial resources necessary for sending their children to key point schools (such as buying or renting an additional property in the area where the school is located and paying for additional tutoring for children).

Conclusion

This chapter considered the motivations and mobilities of three types of host country national teacher: Returners, Reachers, and Remainers. Although each type is qualitatively different from the other, they are nevertheless connected by a pragmatic response to precarity, which includes lacking social connections (*guanxi*), discrimination based on *hukou*, and uncertainty regarding education for children due to unequal access to educational resources.

Having mapped out the journey ahead in Chapter 1 ('Planning'), travelled through the Chinese international school landscape in Chapter 2 ('Departure') and met and listened to the participants in this chapter ('Arrival'), the reader is now ready for the return trip. In the next and final chapter ('Return'), I return to and tie together the insights from the previous three chapters to construct a typology of host country national school teachers. I also consider the significance of the typology for current and future research and end this book by offering an agenda for future research.

References

Bailey, L. (2015). Reskilled and "running ahead": Teachers in an international school talk about their work. *Journal of Research in International Education, 14*(1), 3–15.

Bailey, L. (2021). International school teachers: Precarity during the COVID-19 pandemic. *Journal of Global Mobility: The Home of Expatriate Management Research, 9*(1), 31–43.

BBC (2013, June). What does Xi Jinping's China Dream mean? *BBC News.* www.bbc.com/news/world-asia-china-22726375

Bickenbach, F., & Liu, W. H. (2022). Goodbye China: What do fewer foreigners mean for multinationals and the Chinese economy? *Intereconomics, 57*(5), 306–312.

Bourdieu, P. (1990). *The logic of practice*. Polity Press.

Bright, D. (2022). Understanding why Western expatriate teachers choose to work in non-traditional international schools in Vietnam. *Teachers and Teaching, 28*(5), 633–647.

Bunnell, T. (2016). Teachers in international schools: A global educational "precariat"? *Globalisation, Societies and Education, 14*(4), 543–559.

Canterford, G. (2003). Segmented labour markets in international schools. *Journal of Research in International Education, 2*(1), 47–65.

Centre for China and Globalization (CCG). (2017). Attracting skilled international migrants to China: A review and comparison of policies and practices. *Centre for China and Globalization.* www.ilo.org/wcmsp5/groups/public/-asia/-ro-bangkok/-ilo-beijing/documents/publication/wcms_570674.pdf

Chou, M. H. (2021). Sticky and slippery destinations for academic mobility: The case of Singapore. *Higher Education, 82*(4), 749–764.

Coleman, A. (2022). *Class, place, and higher education: Experiences of homely mobility*. Bloomsbury Publishing.

Cutri, J. E. (2022). *The localisation of Australian elite education within China: A case-study of various social actors' experiences at a Sino-Australian senior school* [Doctoral thesis, Monash University]. https://doi.org/10.26180/21323604.v1

Du, Z., Sun, Y., Zhao, G., & Zweig, D. (2021). Do overseas returnees excel in the Chinese labour market? *The China Quarterly, 247*, 875–897.

ERI. (2023). Primary school teacher salary in China. *Economic Research Institute.* www.erieri.com/salary/job/primary-school-teacher/china#:~:text=The%20average%20pay%20for%20a,for%20a%20Primary%20School%20Teacher

Fish, R. J., Parris, D. L., & Troilo, M. (2017). Compound voids and unproductive entrepreneurship: The rise of the "English fever" in China. *Journal of Economic Issues, 51*(1), 163–180. http://doi.org/10.1080/00213624.2017.1287506

Forsberg, S. (2019). "The right to immobility" and the uneven distribution of spatial capital: Negotiating youth transitions in northern Sweden. *Social and Cultural Geography, 20*(3), 323–343.

Hammer, L. L. (2021). *Exploring the ethnic gap in teacher salaries in international schools* [Doctoral thesis, Wilkes University]. Proquest. www.proquest.com/openview/870eda82d9e626ed0bd31833924eaa53/1?pq-origsite=gscholar&cbl=18750&diss=y

Hao, J., & Welch, A. (2012). A tale of sea turtles: Job-seeking experiences of *hai gui* (high-skilled returnees) in China. *Higher Education Policy, 25*, 243–260.

Hao, L., Hu, A., & Lo, J. (2014). Two aspects of the rural-urban divide and educational stratification in China: A trajectory analysis. *Comparative Education Review, 58*(3), 509–536.

Hardman, J. (2001). Improving recruitment and retention of quality overseas teacher. In S. Blandford & M. Shaw (Eds.), *Managing international schools* (pp. 123–135). Routledge Falmer.

Hatch, J. (2020). The elephant in the room? *International School Magazine.* https://issuu.com/williamclarence/docs/is_mag_22.2/s/10785783

He, N. (2011). Money, fraud and *hukou*. *China Daily.* www.chinadaily.com.cn/2011-07/11/content_12871956.htm

Ibrahim, A. (2020). How Xi Jinping is ruining China's dream of a century of dominance. *The National Interest.* https://nationalinterest.org/blog/buzz/how-xi-jinping-ruining-chinas-dream-century-dominance-163331

Jiang, S. (2021). The call of the homeland: Transnational education and the rising nationalism among Chinese overseas students. *Comparative Education Review*, *65*(1), 34–55.

Lee, D. S. (2019). China's K-12 teacher qualification system. *Jurnal Penelitian dan Evaluasi Pendidikan*, *23*(1), 76–86.

Li, Q., Zhu, X., & Lo, L. N. (2019). Teacher education and teaching in China. *Teachers and Teaching*, *25*(7), 753–756.

Liang, X., Kidwai, H., Zhang, M., & Zhang, Y. (2016). How Shanghai does it: Insights and lessons from the highest-ranking education system in the world. *World Bank Publications*. https://documents1.worldbank.org/curated/ar/643091467988910949/pdf/How-Shanghai-does-it-insights-and-lessons-from-the-highest-ranking-education-system-in-the-world.pdf

Lo, L. N. (2019). Teachers and teaching in China: A critical reflection. *Teachers and Teaching*, *25*(5), 553–573.

Looker, E. D., & Naylor, T. D. (2009). "At risk" of being rural? The experience of rural youth in a risk society. *Journal of Rural and Community Development*, *4*(2), 39–64.

Machin, D. (2021). We need to talk about pay inequality in international schools. *School Management Plus*. www.schoolmanagementplus.com/international-schools/we-need-to-talk-about-pay-inequality-in-international-schools/

MacLachlan, I., & Gong, Y. (2022). China's new age floating population: Talent workers and drifting elders. *Cities*, *131*, 103960.

Maire, Q. (2022). International capital and social class: A sociology of international certification in French urban school markets. *British Journal of Sociology of Education*, *43*(8), 1175–1195.

Mansfield, D. (2022). How reforms have affected British schools in China. *TES Magazine*. www.tes.com/magazine/analysis/specialist-sector/how-reforms-have-affected-british-schools-china

Miao, L., Zheng, J., Jean, J. A., & Lu, Y. (2022). China's international talent policy (ITP): The changes and driving forces, 1978–2020. *Journal of Contemporary China*, *31*(136), 644–661.

Poole, A. (2019). International education teachers' experiences as an educational precariat in China. *Journal of Research in International Education*, *18*(1), 60–76.

Poole, A. (2022). More than interchangeable "local" teachers: Host country teachers' journeys into internationalised school teaching in China. *Research in Comparative and International Education*, *17*(3), 424–440.

Poole, A., & Bunnell, T. (2021). Developing the notion of teaching in "international schools" as precarious: Towards a more nuanced approach based upon "transition capital". *Globalisation, Societies and Education*, *19*(3), 287–297.

Poole, A., & Bunnell, T. (2023). Teachers in "international schools" as an emerging field of inquiry: A literature review of themes and theoretical developments. *Compare: A Journal of Comparative and International Education*. https://doi.org/10.1080/03057925.2023.2212110

Qian, W. (2007). What kinds of overseas talents does China needs? *China.org*. www.china.org.cn/english/education/196881.htm

Ravn, S. (2022). Reframing immobility: Young women aspiring to "good enough" local futures. *Journal of Youth Studies*, *25*(9), 1236–1250.

Rey, J., Bolay, M., & Gez, Y. N. (2020). Precarious privilege: Personal debt, lifestyle aspirations and mobility among international school teachers. *Globalisation, Societies and Education*, *18*(4), 361–373.

Schewel, K. (2020). Understanding immobility: Moving beyond the mobility bias in migration studies. *International Migration Review, 54*(2), 328–355.

Tai, M. (2017). China's tough job market is creating more postgrads. *Nikkei Asia.* https://asia.nikkei.com/Economy/China-s-tough-job-market-is-creating-more-postgrads

Wu, B. (2021). Research on the impact of China's "double reduction" policy on out-of-school remedial classes. In *2021 3rd international conference on economic management and cultural industry (ICEMCI 2021)* (pp. 548–552). Atlantis Press.

Wu, Q., & Wallace, M. (2021). *Hukou* stratification, class structure, and earnings in transitional China. *Chinese Sociological Review, 53*(3), 223–253.

Xiao, C., & Wang, X. (2022). Overseas Chinese returnees' swindler syndrome and their entrepreneurial education under psychological resilience. *Frontiers in Psychology, 12*, 5961.

Yang, L., Xie, Y., Zhou, A., Zhang, W., & Smith, J. (2023). The impact of the implementation of "double reduction" policy on tutors in shadow education: Legislation goals and early experiences. *Compare: A Journal of Comparative and International Education*, 1–17.

Yao, M. (2022). Graduate school, work, or unclear? Gender differences in post-college plans among China's recent college students. *Sociological Perspectives*, 07311214221124536.

Yemini, M., & Maxwell, C. (2018). De-coupling or remaining closely coupled to "home": Educational strategies around identity-making and advantage of Israeli global middle-class families in London. *British Journal of Sociology of Education, 39*(7), 1030–1044. https://doi.org/10.1080/01425692.2018.1454299

Young, N. A. (2018). Departing from the beaten path: International schools in China as a response to discrimination and academic failure in the Chinese educational system. *Comparative Education, 54*(2), 159–180.

Zeng, X. L. (2021). Vocational education – removing the stigma. *China Daily.* www.chinadaily.com.cn/a/202110/15/WS61690e96a310cdd39bc6f350.html

Zhong, Y. M. (2023). The Chinese Double Reduction policy: Challenges to private and public education systems. *Cornell Policy Review*, 1–12. www.cornellpolicyreview.com/the-chinese-double-reduction-policy-challenges-to-private-and-public-education-systems/

Zhou, W. T. (2021). Returnees vital to Shanghai's innovation. *China Daily.* https://global.chinadaily.com.cn/a/202110/02/WS6157b215a310cdd39bc6cd8d.html

Zou, S. (2019). Slower rise in Chinese studying overseas. *China Daily.* www.chinadaily.com.cn/a/201904/16/WS5cb5270aa3104842260b65df.html

Zweig, D., & Han, D. (2010). Sea turtles' or "seaweed?" The employment of overseas returnees in China'. *The internationalization of labour markets*, 89–104.

4 Return

Constructing a typology of host country national teachers

Introduction

The insights from Chapter 3 evidence a range of teacher motivation, encompassing intrinsic, altruistic, and extrinsic factors. Ru's narrative, for example, suggested an altruistic motivation to working in international schools, as he found little meaning in his previous career in IT and instead found spiritual meaning working with students. Working in an international school was the most direct way for him to achieve his goal of becoming a teacher, as working in a public school was impossible for him at this time as it required professional qualifications. Shu's narrative, meanwhile, showed evidence of intrinsic motivation. From a young age, Shu wanted to become a teacher but was unable to do so due to issues related to the *hukou* system, as well as limited chances to work as a public school teacher. Working in a tutoring company and then leveraging the pedagogical capital accrued therein, enabled her to secure a position in a prestigious international school in Shanghai and to realise her dream of becoming a teacher, even if her current position was what she disparagingly referred to as 'dummy's English'.

Overall, however, the participants were primarily motivated by extrinsic factors. These extrinsic factors centred on economic and educational benefits for the teachers and their families. This was most vividly illustrated by Ying, who was motivated to work in her international school due to 'convenience' and also because it provided her with a way to access educational advantage which she otherwise would not have been able to access. Even for teachers like Ru and Shu, who were intrinsic and altruistically motivated, international school teaching was still largely pragmatic in nature. For Ru, international school teaching enabled him to establish a rewarding career on his return to China, while for Shu working in an international school provided her with somewhere to live and save for the future.

Based on the insights from Chapter 3, host country national teachers in international schools occupy a precarious yet aspirational position in China's expanding middle class. They may not have had the economic resources that characterise an entrepreneurial class (although many of the participants

DOI: 10.4324/9781003396291-4

demonstrated an entrepreneurial spirit), but they were able to leverage other, more symbolic resources, such as their 'international' and 'mobility' capital, which could be converted to economic capital at a later date (perhaps through their children's own educational journey via international schooling and on to an overseas university). The teachers' precarious position as an emerging *xiaokang* thus shaped their motivations for working in international schools.

I next 'return' to the international school literature surveyed in Chapter 1 to consider how the participants' motivations compare with those of other host country national teachers, teachers in public schools in China, expatriate international school teachers, and parents. I then use the insights from Chapter 3 to construct a typology of host country national teachers and explain how the typology relates, and extends, to existing international school teacher typologies, and how the typology might be used by researchers.

Returning to the academic literature

Motivation and host country national teachers

There are relatively few studies on host country national teachers and even fewer on host country national teachers and motivation. Therefore, relating the insights from this book to previous research is not an easy task. However, one study that does focus on host country national teachers' motivations and experiences is Hammer's (2021) study on split salaries in international schools. Hammer's study employed semi-structured interviewing with ten host country national teachers who worked in various international schools – for example Type A, B, or C (Hayden & Thompson, 2013) – around the world in order to explore the issue of split salaries (whereby expatriate teachers are paid more than host country national teachers). Three key themes emerged: power, othering, and the cost of compromise. As part of the theme of power, the participants talked about why they chose to work in an international school. Their responses resonate with some of the insights from Chapter 3. Hammer found that the participants were motivated to work in an international school because of career-building, better working conditions, and, most germane to the participants in this book, increased social capital – that is the networks of friends, colleagues, and acquaintances that individuals can mobilise to achieve status and better opportunities (Bailey, 2021, cited in Hammer, 2021, p. 67).

The participants in this book were similarly motivated by extrinsic factors, thereby suggesting that host country national teachers tend to adopt a pragmatic orientation to teaching in international schools. However, the nature of the extrinsic motivation is somewhat different. Whereas the teachers in Hammer's study considered the cultivation of social capital to be an initial motivator, the participants in this book appeared to be less motivated to develop connections and more motivated to accrue benefits. This was particularly the case for Remainers (teachers who were married, had children, and were largely immobile), who were able to use their position as teachers to access and pass on intergenerational advantage to their children. The reason for this difference may be explained by the unequal and inequitable nature of China's educational landscape, as well as the participants' precarious position as an emerging *xiaokang* in China's fragmented and highly stratified middle class.

Motivation and public school teachers in China

The participants' largely extrinsic motivation appears to be at odds with how teaching is generally perceived in China. It has been observed that teachers in China should, among other things, model good moral character and love and be dedicated to the teaching profession (Ye et al., 2022). The participants, in contrast, did not profess love for teaching, as they emphasised extrinsic factors. This difference may be due to the nature of public and private schooling in China. Public school teaching might be thought of as more of a vocation, as teachers choose this profession early in their careers. Moreover, teachers in public schools may be more altruistically motivated as they enjoy more stability than teachers in private international schooling and therefore have the luxury to focus on making a difference in their students' life. It might also be the case that the 'moral' dimension of teaching in China is now more of an ideal than a reality, with studies starting to identify the kinds of extrinsic motivation and pragmatism articulated by the participants working in private international schools. For example, several studies on teachers' profession-entry motivation in China (Su et al., 2001; Lin et al., 2012) have shown that far from being dedicated to the profession because of love, teachers are increasingly drawn to the profession because of extrinsic factors, with China's status as a developing nation offered as a reason for the impact of socio-economic determinants on teachers' motivation (Bukhari et al., 2023).

Motivation and expatriate teachers

To a certain extent, host country national teachers' reasons and motivations for working in international schools reflect those of their expatriate counterparts. Previous studies (e.g. Bright, 2022; Hrycak, 2015; Soong & Stahl, 2021) have emphasised extrinsic factors such as benefits, status, and money. Of particular relevance is Tarc et al.'s (2019) study of Canadian international school teachers which found that the participants used their positions so their children could gain access to an elite international education, thereby furthering their class-making trajectories. Significantly, some of the participants in this book (Reacher teachers such as Ying) also utilised their positions as international school teachers to expand their repertoires of school choice and thereby realise intergenerational social advantage for their children.

While the literature on expatriate teacher motivation does emphasise extrinsic factors, as previously highlighted, there is also evidence of intrinsic and even altruistic motivations (e.g. Dos Santos, 2019; Bailey, 2015; Lee et al., 2022; Savva, 2013). For example, Bailey and Cooker's (2019) typology of international school teachers includes all three forms of motivations. Type A teachers are intrinsically drawn to international school teaching as it facilitates mobility and adventure. Type B teachers are altruistically drawn to international school teaching as they view it as a way for them to make a difference to their students' lives and to change the world in global and ideological ways. Type C teachers might be said to be both intrinsically and extrinsically drawn to international school teaching. In terms of the former, they may be motivated to remain 'closely coupled to home' (Yemini & Maxwell, 2018) due to personal interest, while in terms of the latter, they may elect to be immobile due to family reasons, suggesting a more pragmatic orientation to motivation.

The reason for the differences between expatriate and host country national teacher motivations is multifaceted in nature, implicating a range of sociocultural factors. While expatriate teachers in international schools in China can face discrimination and the marginalisation of their professional identities (Bunnell & Poole, 2022), they are able to transition from school to school relatively easily due to their qualifications and white skin privilege (Poole, 2022b). Host country national teachers, in contrast, may be able to fall back on local support networks in times of crisis, but their ability to be mobile is more circumscribed than their expatriate counterparts, who constitute a global middle class (Ball & Nakita, 2014) – that is professionals and their families who move around the globe. While host country national teachers are by no means 'sedentary' (Rey et al., 2020), with some of the participants electing to be mobile to overcome structural barriers, their potential to be mobile (their motility) is nevertheless limited to internal migration throughout China due to their personal circumstances. Rather than viewing these teachers as less mobile, it would be more productive to view them as being mobile 'differently' (Wu & Koh, 2022), thereby legitimating a plurality of mobilities, including the symbolic, imaginary, and anticipatory (i.e. sending a child to an international school, which will subsequently facilitate global mobility), as well as strategic forms of immobility, such as 'spatial continuity' (Schewel, 2020).

Another sociocultural factor that needs to be considered in explaining the contrasting motivations of expatriate and host country national teachers is China's status as a developing nation. China may have lifted millions of people out of poverty and expanded its middle class, but the middle class remains highly stratified and precarious as China still lacks a social security net if individuals fall into unemployment. Generally, Chinese families still tend to rely on the transfer of intergenerational wealth as a safety net. For host country national teachers, such precarity is likely to be exacerbated by a range of institutional (such as the practice of hiring teachers on short-term contracts); policy (such as the Double Reduction Policy and the regulation of the international school sector); and global (such as the impact of COVID-19) factors, all of which have created considerable uncertainly and disruption to the lives of citizens and residents in China.

Given this existential precarity, it is little wonder that host country national teachers are extrinsically motivated. Can they be blamed for wanting to work in international schools not because of some intrinsic reason connected to teaching or making the world a better place but because of the material and symbolic advantages it affords them and their families? Certainly not. Intrinsic and altruistic motivations are only likely to flourish in contexts where teachers do not need to fight for survival or compete for scarce educational resources. However, such a situation does not preclude the development of greater pedagogical engagement once teachers (hopefully) become more stable and settle into their careers. Teachers' ongoing motivation to remain working in international schools may be a space where intrinsic, and perhaps even altruistic, motivation might be cultivated. This is something that I return to later in this chapter when I consider the implications of the insights from Chapter 3 for the creation of a teaching qualification tailored to host country national teachers' motivations and mobilities.

A final reason for the differing motivations of expatriate and host country national teachers may be due to the privileging of the expatriate teacher experience (Poole & Bunnell, 2023), which has rendered host country national teachers' experiences and involvement in international schooling marginal at best. It may very well be the case that host country national teachers in China are intrinsically motivated, but they have yet to be explored in sufficient depth for this to be revealed. Moreover, the approach taken for this book may have also restricted the kinds of motivation the teachers were able to articulate. The interviews, for example, focused primarily on the teachers' initial motivations and did not offer much scope for the investigation of their ongoing motivation. This is something that future research would need to investigate further.

Motivation and parents

The insights from this book also reflect findings from the study of parental motivation in relation to international schools in China (e.g. Cutri, 2022; Ma & Wright, 2021; Young, 2018; Wright et al., 2022), as well as internationally, such as Thailand (Namraksa & Kraiwanit, 2023), Cyprus (Hagage Baikovich & Yemini, 2022), and Kuwait (Khalil & Kelly, 2020). To a lesser extent, the insights from this book also resonate with middle-class parents' class-making strategies more generally (e.g. Maxwell & Yemini, 2019; Yemini & Maxwell, 2018). For example, Young's (2018) study of precarious middle-class parents found that international schools function as a kind of backup plan of sorts, offering a second chance to students who had underperformed or faced discrimination in the public school system, which, as noted in Chapter 3, is highly competitive. Interestingly, working in international schools (or their current international school) was not the participants' first choice. Rather, they migrated into international schooling from other careers (such as university teaching or private tutoring) or ended up working in an international school when their first career choice was impossible to realise. This was most vividly seen in Shu's narrative, where, after being unable to become a public school teacher, she found her way into international school teaching.

The similar responses to teacher and parental motivations for engaging in international schooling suggest that the ontological distinction between parent and teacher is not as discrete as many have assumed. Moreover, in the case of some of the participants in this book (e.g. Ying, Jin, Gang, and Mei), it is possible to discern a hybrid identity position that encompasses both teacher and parent. While some previous studies, such as Tarc et al. (2019), have explored teachers who use their position as international school teachers to transmit advantage to their children, the participants in this book were not so much 'teachers who are parents' but rather 'parents who were teachers'. This is because being a parent and seeking to accrue advantage for their child(ren) appeared to be the primary motivator for many of the participants, although it is likely that over time host country national teachers will become more teacher-oriented and therefore transition to an identity position of 'teacher who is a parent'. The insights from this book suggest that the categories of teacher and parent are in need of being brought together in order to understand the lived experiences of host country national teachers.

A typology of host country national teachers

Using the participants' motivations and prior experiences from Chapter 3, I present a typology of host country national school teachers in international schools in China (henceforth simply referred to as the typology). Table 4.1 summarises the typology.

Before discussing the typology in more detail, it is necessary to highlight a number of caveats. While the typology assigns teachers to a specific type, it is likely that teachers will change type over time. This is indeed acknowledged by Bailey and Cooker (2019) and Rey et al. (2020) and is also evident within the narratives of some of the participants. For example, Gang started out as a Remainer teacher who was motivated to work in the school 'on the doorstep' but later transitioned to a Reacher teacher by becoming more mobile. Shu's experiences also show similar mobility between types. While she is a Reacher teacher, in that she sees international school teaching as a way to foster greater social mobility, there is evidence of her using international school teaching to be more strategically immobile, therefore suggesting that she aspires to be a Remainer.

Compounding matters is the fact that teachers can occupy multiple types simultaneously. For example, Ying was *a priori* a Remainer as she was 'closely coupled to home' (Yemini & Maxwell, 2018) due to marriage and family, yet she could also be seen as a Reacher, as working in an international school enabled her to access educational resources (e.g. an international curriculum) and social/symbolic capital (access to an over-sea's university) could

Table 4.1 Typology of host country national teachers.

Type	Definition	Motivation	Key concepts
Returners	Returners possess 'international capital', which is valued by international school recruiters, but often lack pedagogical and social capital	Some evidence of altruistic motivation, but Returners are largely motivated to work in the international school sector as it provides them with a re-entry point into the Chinese labour force	*Haigui* International, pedagogical, and social capital
Reachers	Internal migrants who possess pedagogical capital but may lack international capital	Some evidence of intrinsic motivation, but Reachers tend to use international school teaching to foster social mobility and overcome structural barriers created by the *hukou* system	Teacher profession *Hukou*
Remainers	Remainers may possess international capital and have an attachment to the locale due to family and children and are therefore relatively immobile	Motivation is primarily extrinsic in nature, with Remainers using their position as teachers to engage in school choice for their children	Immobility Spatial continuity *Xiaokang*

be mobilised for her children's benefit. Meanwhile, Ru was considered to be a Returner as his overseas experiences primarily shaped his journey into international schooling. However, he could also be said to be a Remainer, as his school was located in Beijing where his family lived.

With the above caveats in mind, the typology is primarily based on teachers' initial motivations for working in international schools and therefore may not yield insights into their ongoing motivation. This is discussed in more detail a little later on when I suggest how the typology might be used by researchers.

How the typology relates to the international school literature

The typology adds to previous international school teacher typologies and research in a number of ways. Table 4.2 summarises these previous typologies (the reader can also find a more detailed discussion of them in Chapter 1).

Table 4.2 Summary of international school teacher typologies.

Author	Teacher types
Garton (2000)	*Host country nationals* – teachers whose nationality is the same as that of the school *Local hire expatriates* – teachers hired in country and who typically do not receive all benefits *Overseas hire expatriates* – teachers hired from outside the country who typically receive full benefits
Hardman (2001)	*Career professionals* – teachers who are dedicated and more likely to get involved with students and student activities. *Penelopes* – teachers who are faithful to the country they have adopted even after they have outlived their value *Mavericks* – a global traveller or someone seeking to escape from national constraints and other issues in their home country
Bailey and Cooker (2019)	*Type A teachers* – see teaching as a way to support travel and mobility *Type B teachers* – commit to the profession because it enables them to make a difference to students' lives: to change the world in global, ideological ways *Type C teachers* – view their primary attachment as being to the locale in which the international school is situated
Rey et al. (2020)	*The expat* – foreign teachers whose mobility is tied to personal circumstances, most commonly by travelling with one's partner and family as a 'trailing spouse' *The adventurer* – typically white, trained teachers from Anglo-Saxon countries and are mostly young and unaccompanied by spouse or children; teaching is a means to mobility *The local* – teachers from a local background who are usually trained within their country and have transitioned to an international school from the public or private sector

national teachers' motivations and mobilities. As reiterated throughout this book, the literature has tended to focus on the expatriate teacher (e.g. Bailey & Cooker, 2019; Hardman, 2001) or treated the host country national teacher as a discrete category (e.g. Garton, 2000; Rey et al., 2020). The typology does not simply offer one overarching homogenous category but offers three types of host country national teachers based on their initial motivation for working in international schools. The insights from Chapter 3 also demonstrated that host county national teachers cannot always 'simply' transition from public schools to international schools due to structural barriers that can frustrate and preclude such transitioning.

Second, the typology expands Bailey and Cooker's (2019) Type C teacher label. For example, the notion of the Remainer teacher resonates with the Type C teacher, as both elect to be 'closely coupled to home' (Yemini & Maxwell,

2018). Moreover, Bailey and Cooker's (2019) notion of the 'Accidental Teacher' resonates with Returner, Remainer, and Reacher teachers alike. Accidental teachers are teachers who did not set out to be teachers but fell into international school teaching through happenstance and, as the participants frequently put it, 'coincidence'. In the case of the teachers in this study, however, it might be more accurate to describe them as 'Accidental international school teachers'. This is because many of them had prior teaching experiences in other educational contexts, such as the private tutoring industry and higher education, and only later worked in an international school teaching or did not set out to become international school teachers at the start of their careers. Therefore, it is necessary to make a distinction between 'international school teachers' and 'teachers in international schools'.

Whereas the 'international school teacher' label might be seen as both an academic (Poole & Bunnell, 2023) and identity construct (based on beliefs and intrinsic motivations), the label 'teacher in an international school' does not consider the nature of the school itself to be that significant in shaping a teacher's identity. The participants in this book would best be described as 'teachers in international schools' as they did not articulate any intrinsic desire to teach internationally nor did they define themselves as international school teachers. They were teachers who happened to work in international schools. In fact, some of the participants in other interviews considered the only difference between public schools and private international schools in China to be curricular in nature. Gang, for example, felt that 'the only difference from domestic high schools is that when the final exam is held, one is a foreign paper, and the other is a domestic paper', although he also acknowledged that students in international schools were 'bolder, more innovative, less conformist, and more personal' than their domestic counterparts. It could very well be that host country national teachers may start their international school careers as 'teachers in international schools' and then later transition to being 'international school teachers' once they have settled into the role and developed professionally. This would necessitate the adoption by researchers of both sociological lenses, as well as identity related ones, such as teacher professional identity.

The typology also adds to the scholarship on host country national teachers and mobility. The insights from this book indicate that host country national teachers are more mobile – or mobile in more complex and different ways – than previous research has suggested. As noted throughout this book, host country national teachers are often differentiated from expatriate teachers on the basis of their motility, with a lack of mobility being negatively equated with being left behind or stuck. However, this creates something of a false dichotomy, thereby positioning expatriate teachers as the positive pole of the host country–expatriate teacher dichotomy (due to the positive connotation of being mobile) and relegating host country national teachers to the negative pole, due to the assumption that they are inherently immobile and the assumption that immobility is undesirable. The mobility discourse on host country national teachers appears to be framed in terms of a 'sedentary metanarrative' (Schewel, 2020) that presumes being immobile as normal (and also a feature of a specific type of teacher), promoting mobility, which is considered to be exceptional or different, to the forefront of analysis. As argued in Chapter 3, mobility scholars have started to advance a research agenda which frames immobility as equally as complex, dynamic, and diverse as moving (Schewel, 2020). This agenda needs to be adopted by international school researchers and applied to the study of international school teachers generally and host country national teachers specifically.

Far from being 'sedentary' (Rey et al., 2020), the participants in this book were relatively mobile, with some, such as Gang, 'jumping' from one school to another. And even when the participants were immobile, such as Ying, they were still able to engage in symbolic or anticipated mobility, using the educational resources 'on the doorstep' to lay the foundations for their family's future social mobility. While host country national teachers are more immobile than their expatriate counterparts and, indeed, may aspire to become 'closely coupled to home' (Yemini & Maxwell, 2018) in the long term, this should not obscure the many ways in which host country teachers are mobile, often engaging in short-term mobility and embracing precarity in order to realise a more immobile and stable future. These teachers should be understood as being mobile 'differently' (Wu & Koh, 2022) and this difference needs to be acknowledged by scholars.

Having outlined the main insights of this book, how they have been used to create a typology, and how it complements and extends previous scholarship, I next consider how the typology might be used in future research, underscoring the need to consider the ethical dimension of typologising and research more generally which still tends to emphasise ontological and epistemological dimensions.

Ethics of typologising (necessary digression # 2)

In earlier papers (e.g. Poole, 2020, 2022a), I adopted a critical stance towards the nature and application of teacher typologies, which coalesced around a three-pronged ontological, epistemological, and ethical critique. I considered typologies incapable of capturing what I described as the 'resonant live sound of lived experience' (Poole, 2021, p. x). That is, if we are to really understand teachers and their identities, we needed to attend to their lived experiences, which are inherently complex and contradictory. The typology could only offer a snapshot of lived experience, as it reified lived experience, reducing the complex to two-dimensional caricature. For me, the typology was akin to a kind of qualitative betrayal. As such, I considered previous typologies (e.g. Garton, 2000; Hardman, 2001; Bailey & Cooker, 2019; Rey et al., 2020) to contravene the sanctity of lived experience.

Since then, my stance towards the typology has softened, partly influenced by the writing of this book, as well as recent contributions to the academic literature (e.g. Bright, 2022), which have sought to strike a balance between deductive and inductive approaches. Now, I have come to see that it is not the typology in and of itself that is the issue but rather how it is used. Significantly, international school scholars (e.g. Hardman, 2001; Bailey & Cooker, 2019; Rey et al., 2020) remain silent on the issue of the ethics of typologising and educational research more generally. They may highlight the limitation of the typology, such as Rey et al. (2020, p. 371) observation that teachers 'may shift categories along their professional trajectory' or Bailey and Cooker's (2019, p. 137) acknowledgement that 'teachers can change between the categories too', but these reflections are primarily ontological and methodological in nature. Ethical considerations and how the typology should be used by researchers have yet to be addressed.

The reason for this silence may be that notions of ethics are still largely conceived as what happens before research gets going, with statements of ethics all too frequently aping the prescriptive and generic credo of 'do no harm'. Once ethical approval has been granted, researchers may consider ethics to no longer be of relevance to data collection, analysis, and dissemination. Another reason may be due to lingering positivist notions of rigour. As scholars are required to demonstrate rigour, qualitative researchers need to spend a good chunk of their word count appeasing the (often) positivist reader and assuaging their doubts about qualitative research as lacking rigour, thereby leaving little space for the consideration of ethics. Even in a qualitative paradigm, ethics becomes subordinated to ontology as the latter is still taken to be foundational.

Increasingly, qualitative researchers have started to argue that researchers need to be more active in the research process, with ethics being understood as a reciprocal relationship between researcher and participant(s) that needs to be continually renegotiated as the research progresses (Clandinin, 2016; Pollard, 2015). The typology is a powerful form of data and, due to its scientific lineage, has about it a certain smug objectivity; once the interview data are sifted, purged, and pulped into the sleek and shiny typology, the relational, human aspect, is all too easily lost. With these issues in mind, it is necessary to consider not just the what of research but, more importantly, the how. How is the typology to be used? To what end? What is missing is how the typology should be used, thereby necessitating the inclusion of an ethics of typologising to the dialogue. In what follows, I offer some guidelines for the application of the typology, stating what it can and, most crucially, cannot do.

First, the typology is prospective in nature. It is designed as a heuristic or a starting point for further research. The typology is not designed to be used 'scientifically'. It does not form a self-contained whole but is a work in progress. I do not see the typology, for example, being used in the same manner as Hayden and Thompson's (2013) tripartite typology of international schools. The typology is presented as a conversation in an ongoing dialogue. It might be thought of as a conversation starter, which other scholars are encouraged to continue. The typology itself, of course, needs to be well constructed and the process by which it was constructed needs to be articulated in a transparent manner. However, for me, the typology can only be 'valid' if used tentatively (e.g. host country teachers may be x, y, and z), and ethically (e.g. giving voice or inspiring research into marginalised groups). Some may argue that these qualifications devalue the significance of the typology. This may be true from a purely positivist perspective; however, from a social justice perspective, the value of the typology lies in giving voice to host country national teachers and (it is hoped) inspiring future research into the experiences of these teachers.

Second, the typology is designed to be used in conjunction with other research methods, particularly in-depth interviewing. As mentioned earlier, researchers could use the typology to initially identify different types of teachers based on their motivations and mobilities, which would then need to be refined by further rounds of data collection and analysis. The typology, then, could be used deductively to differentiate between different types of host country national teachers and construct interview questions. Subsequent rounds of inductive analysis would then complexify the typology by refining and expanding it to include other types of teachers, motivations, and mobilities.

Third, the typology is designed to offer 'fuzzy generalisation' at best. 'Fuzzy generalisation' holds that educational research can be generalised to a certain extent, but such generalisations need to be tentatively formulated to the effect that the same relationship may be found in other cases (Bassey, 2001). With this in mind, even though the typology is based on the motivations and mobilities of Chinese host country national teachers, it may have applicability to host country teachers in other countries and contexts. For example, teachers in other developing Asia-Pacific countries, such as Vietnam, Thailand, and the Philippines, may fall into the same categories, due to similar socio-economic issues (i.e. expanding middle class and educational inequity). For host country national teachers in developed countries, the typology may not be as relevant, but its design and use may still be of use to researchers. It is hoped that the typology inspires other researchers to construct typologies of their own. More research is needed on teachers in other types of international school (e.g. Type A traditional schools), as well as their initial and ongoing motivations and professional development needs.

Implications for professional accreditation of teachers

The findings from this book also have implications for the professional accreditation of host country national teachers. The reader may wish to read/ re-read Chapter 2 before engaging with the implications section, as much of what follows assumes contextual understanding of the regulation of the international school sector. Specially, I focus on private schools that cater for Chinese citizens, which I refer to throughout as 'internationalised schools'.

Prior to the 2021 government regulation of the international school sector in China, internationalised schools in China did not require incoming teachers to hold formal teaching qualifications. First, the demand for private internationalised schooling was (and perhaps still is) such that demand from middle-class consumers outstripped supply (Gaskell, 2019). Significantly, it had been argued that the majority of foreign teachers in China were unqualified (Quinn, 2019). The insights from this book suggest that host country national teachers are also likely to be similarly unqualified (i.e. lacking pedagogical capital). At the same time, it is also necessary to recognise that there will be host country national teachers who do hold teaching qualifications, perhaps because they have transitioned from public to international school teaching or they have been teaching in international schools for some time.

With the introduction of government regulation, it is likely that teachers (both local and expatriate) entering internationalised schools will need to hold a teaching qualification. What 'qualified' means within the context of international schooling in China and other countries remains fuzzy, not least of all because the adjective 'international' is highly ambiguous. Would teachers need to be similarly qualified as their counterparts in state-run schools? Would being qualified in an internationalised school require understanding of additional components related to an international dimension, such as global competence or intercultural awareness? These questions cannot be answered here, but it is certainly worth considering what a teaching qualification tailored to host country national teachers in internationalised schools might look like.

Currently, there are a number of qualifications tailored to host country national teachers that could serve as inspiration. One example is 'PGCE-China' offered by Buckingham International School of Education, which, according to the course description, is aimed at China-based teachers who are looking to complete a 'demanding' British teaching course and to develop the understanding, pedagogy skills, and competencies needed to be successful in any classroom around the world (BISE, 2023).

There are also a number of other courses that are not specifically designed for China but are nonetheless popular choices for teachers in China. These include Cambridge English (2023) and Cambridge Assessment International Education's (2023) range of general teaching-focused courses, including the Certificate in English Language Teaching – Primary and Secondary (CELT P and S), the Professional Development Qualification – Teaching and Learning (PDQ), and the Teaching Knowledge Test (TKT), as well as shorter, subject-specific certificates.

The CELT P and S is designed for early career English language teachers who have a basic understanding of teaching and learning but are not yet autonomous. The courses aim to help participants improve the quality of their classroom practice by developing and extending their knowledge and skills with fundamental pedagogical principles, such as formative assessment, classroom management, and differentiation.

The PDQ, meanwhile, aims to support teachers to enhance the quality of their students' learning, develop critical engagement with key education theories and concepts, and focus on effective and reflective practice to promote active learning. The qualification contains theoretical, practical, and research components. The PDQ is also offered by The University of Nottingham, Ningbo, which is licensed by Cambridge International to deliver PDQ courses.

Finally, the TKT is a series of modular teaching qualifications which test teachers' knowledge in specific areas of English language teaching, including lesson planning, using resources, and managing the teaching and learning process. The reader can find more information about these courses by consulting some of my other works on their implementation and impact in China (Poole, 2023; Poole & Li, 2023).

The IBO (2023) also offer a range of courses, which are well suited for teachers in international schools. These courses include the IB certificate in teaching and learning (examining the principles and practices associated with one of three IB programmes [Primary Years, Middle Years and Diploma Programmes]); the IB advanced certificate in teaching and learning research (allowing participants to supplement their existing IB experience with investigative work to broaden their knowledge and experience), various leadership certificates (e.g. IB certificate in leadership practice and IB advanced certificate in leadership research), as well as subject-specific certificates that cover aspects such as content and assessment. While these qualifications are likely to be taken by teachers in IB World Schools, they also have applicability to teachers working in Cambridge curriculum schools, as they offer valuable insights regarding notions of intercultural understanding, which has been seen as a cornerstone of any international curriculum.

Towards a teaching qualification for host country national teachers

Taking these qualifications as inspiration and drawing on the insights from this book, I next offer recommendations for the design of a teaching qualification for host country national teachers. The following is not designed as a curriculum as such but rather sets out as a series of imperatives that researchers, school leaders, and educational designers are encouraged to consider when considering how to develop, or localise, a qualification for host country national teachers.

Acknowledge and draw on teachers' lived experiences

A qualification tailored to host country national teachers should be rooted in their lived experiences. Rather than constructing a qualification based on an idealised learner who is both intrinsically and altruistically motivated, it would be necessary to meet the teachers where they are. As the insights from this book suggest, the teachers occupy a position of precarious privilege (Rey et al., 2019), where they combine the advantages of being part of China's middle class with struggling to find a foothold in the Chinese labour market or, if parents, to access educational advantage for their children. Therefore, school leaders and course designers should be mindful of the lived realities that host country national teachers bring with them.

Rather than viewing the teachers through a deficit lens in terms of what they lack, it would be necessary for school leaders to consider what the teachers do in fact bring with them. This might be done through identity work, which I explain in more detail next. At the very least, the curriculum should not just be calibrated to the teachers' pedagogical needs but aim to move beyond this to acknowledge their complex journeys into international schooling. Teachers may become alienated from their learning if they cannot locate themselves within in a curriculum that is divorced from their lived realities and incorrectly calibrated to an idealised, intrinsically motivated teacher. There would need to be incremental movement towards the 'international' that transits teachers from their lived realities – informed by extrinsic motivation – to a new reality that paves the way for the construction of a more intrinsically motivated educator.

Simply put, begin by establishing a firm foundation based on lived experience on which intrinsic motivation can be constructed.

Develop teachers' pedagogical capital

A bespoke qualification for host country national teachers would also need to develop teachers' pedagogical capital. The insights from Chapter 3 highlighted that many of the participants possessed ample amounts of international capital but did not necessarily possess corresponding pedagogical capital or the kinds of pedagogical capital perceived as commensurate with the imperatives of government reform (e.g. greater equity, developing a firm patriotic identity). Even though some of the participants (e.g. Ru, Shu, Jin, and Rong) did possess pedagogical capital derived from their experiences of working in the private tutoring industry, the impact of the Double Reduction Policy has resulted in former tutors struggling to transfer to public school teaching due the stigma of their tutoring experience in private tutoring organisations and not being considered in the recruitment criteria of public school teachers (Yang et al., 2023). Therefore, the impact of government regulation of the international school sector is likely to see the introduction of stricter requirements for teacher recruitment, such as the need for teachers to hold a valid teaching qualification or, at the very least, be working towards one.

Therefore, even if teachers do possess pedagogical capital derived from private tutoring or international school teaching prior to regulation, it may have limited pedagogical and political exchange value in the context of International Schooling 3.0 (see Chapter 2 for a definition of this term). Hence, there may be a need to develop a teaching qualification that will allow teachers to develop new forms of pedagogical capital that is commensurate with the new policy landscape, while also leaving room for the inclusion of aspects that make the qualification more than just a national(ising) teacher qualification.

Simply put, pedagogy should be transformative, but it is also inherently political.

Hybridise pedagogical approaches

Another issue that a teacher qualification for host country national teachers in international school would need to consider is the hybridisation of pedagogical approaches. Generally, two dominant pedagogical approaches tend to be adopted by teachers in China – student-centred and teacher-centred – which are taken to be antithetical. My prior research (e.g. Poole et al., 2022) has found that host country national teachers often struggle to implement student-centred learning approaches due to unfamiliarity and transmissive beliefs about teaching and learning that clash with the constructivist assumptions underpinning student-centred learning (Poole, 2016). Interestingly, my research (e.g. Poole, 2016; Poole et al., 2022) also suggests that expatriate teachers overemphasise student-centred learning, which clashes with the prior educational experiences of Chinese students, whose experiences might be best described as teacher-centred.

These prior studies suggest that a nuanced and balanced approach to teaching and learning approaches is needed and would be commensurate with the hybrid space of the internationalised school. With this in mind, teachers would need to be introduced to the underlying theories of teaching and learning and how they relate to practice. Cambridge's PDQ might serve as inspiration for the content of this module, as it introduces teachers to the main principles and concepts of learning (i.e. constructivism, behaviourism, metacognition, and motivation) and how they relate to teaching practice (lesson planning and lesson observations). The course would be informed by critical pragmatism. Rather than distilling 'effective' education into one approach (e.g. student-centred learning), teachers could be encouraged to construct a toolbox of approaches from which they can draw to meet the needs of a particular topic, lesson, or student.

Simply put, avoid the deification of pedagogy and adopt a pragmatic mind set.

Investigate and construct a philosophy of international education

It would also be necessary to move beyond the pedagogical to consider the underlying philosophy of international education. As this remains highly ambiguous, this process may need to be inductive in nature, with schools constructing their own philosophy and then using it to inform the construction of values, mission, and ethos. This would entail exploring notions of global competence and intercultural understanding. Once again, a course tailored to host country national teachers would need to be based on the needs and realities of the internationalised school. My ongoing research into host country national teachers' understandings of the purpose of international schooling in China has found that teachers often understand the 'international' as rooted in the national or, to put it another way, actors 'exploit "the global" in order to sustain and strengthen the dominance of the nation' (Yemini et al., 2023, p. 4). Such conceptions contrast with those held by expatriate teachers, who often understand the international in transcendental terms which, on closer inspection, betray a Western parochialism masquerading as universalism (Poole, 2017; Van Oord, 2007).

When conceptualising the international, school leaders and course designers could take inspiration from the burgeoning concept of cosmopolitan nationalism. The reader should return to Chapter 2 for a fuller account of this concept, but to summarise here, cosmopolitan nationalism 'captures the complexity and the paradoxical manifestations of such phenomena in different systems' (Yemini et al., 2023, p. 2). The concept returns the nation and the state to the academic conversation about globalisation, but it does so in a way that does not champion 'nationalism' but recognises that internationalisation always involves struggle and tension between the local and the global. This point is particularly significant for international school governance in China, which, as shown by Wright et al. (2022), requires all students to develop a firm patriotic attachment to the state while also providing them with the cosmopolitan tools to engage with the world. In this configuration, cosmopolitanism is not a sensibility but a strategy for national building and the rejuvenation of China.

Simply put, do not assume that the international is *a priori*. Construct it. Localise it.

Develop an international school teacher identity

Finally, a teaching qualification for host country national teachers would also need to engage in identity work. This aspect tends to be missing from the programmes and qualifications explored earlier or only considered to be an outcome. For example, the PDQ's focus on practitioner research encourages teachers to reflect on their experiences and identities, but this is largely an outcome of the course, with little or no reference to the construct of identity or the process of identity work as a solid object of study in terms of content. Teachers could be introduced to different theories of identity and use these to reflect and construct their own identities as international school teachers. Dialogic approaches to identity may be most suitable as they assume a multiple, discontinuous, and social nature of identity, while simultaneously explaining identity as being unitary, continuous, and individual (Akkerman & Meijer, 2011). This might help to transit teachers from being 'teachers in international schools' to 'international school teachers'. Identity work should not form a stand-alone part of the course but needs to be suffused throughout. As part of this pedagogical journey, teachers are likely to transit from being extrinsically motivated to intrinsically motivated, although given the participants' complex circumstances, this should not be an expected outcome of professional learning.

Simply put, make identity work concretely curricular and not just coincidental outcome.

Future journeys

I end this book's journey by considering some new journeys that researchers may wish to take into the emerging phenomenon of host country national teachers in international schools.

First, researchers could consider teachers' ongoing motivations. This book primarily considered host country national teachers' initial motivations for working in international schools. As mentioned at various points throughout this chapter, motivation is a complex and dynamic construct that is likely to change over time and place as individuals move along the life course. Therefore, researchers could consider undertaking a longitudinal investigation into host country national teachers' initial and ongoing motivations in order to ascertain the extent to which motivation changes and the nature of such changes. This may take the form of a comparative longitudinal case study of one, or more, host country national teachers. Connected to this, researchers may wish to consider how motivation correlates with teachers' practice and their attitude towards their professional learning. The typology might be a good place to start regarding this endeavour.

Second, researchers may wish to consider how host country national teachers perceive and negotiate precarity. While this book has emphasised international school teaching as a strategy for moving out of precarity (or at least ameliorating its impact), others (e.g. Bunnell, 2016; Poole, 2019) have argued that teachers in international school may constitute a subgrouping of a global precariat, whose lives are characterised by precarious privilege (Rey et al., 2019; Poole, 2022b). Therefore, future research might consider what types of precarity host country national teachers experience, the extent to which the precarity they experience is similar or different to that experienced by expatriate teachers or teachers in Chinese public schools, and whether host country national teachers are part of a global/Chinese educational precariat.

Third, researchers may wish to consider host country national teachers' identity construction further. Although this book has primarily adopted a sociological framing, a number of identity positionings were identified, including 'international school teachers' versus 'teachers in international schools' and 'teachers as parents' versus 'parents as teachers'. Significantly, the literature has tended to focus on the experiences of teachers and parents as ontologically distinct units of analysis. However, the insights from this book suggest that these two categories can be brought together to understand the lived experiences of host country national teachers with families. Presented here in embryonic form, it is hoped that researchers continue to develop these identity positionings or explore host country national teachers' experiences from the theoretical lens of identity. As mentioned previously, researchers may wish to consider dialogic approaches to identity that assume a multiple, discontinuous, and social nature of identity, while simultaneously explaining identity as being unitary, continuous, and individual (Akkerman & Meijer, 2011). Host country national teachers, therefore, may not embody one core identity – for example teacher as parent – but may transit between 'teacher as parent' and 'parent as teacher' identity positions over time and place, depending on the contexts they find themselves in.

Fourth, researchers may wish to utilise the typology offered in this chapter as a framework for understanding the lived experiences of host country national teachers. Although the typology is based on three types of teachers – Returners, Reachers, and Remainers – it is likely that researchers will identify different types of teachers based on the unit of analysis (i.e. motivation, mobility, lived experience, or practice), the type of school (i.e. traditional vs. non-traditional), and location (rural vs. urban; China vs. outside of China). As pointed out earlier, the typology is designed as a heuristic, so it is hoped that new concepts and insights will emerge from its application. Researchers could consider the extent to which the typology is applicable to teachers in other educational contexts (e.g. public school teaching), as well as other countries. Although the typology has emerged from the lived experiences of host country national teachers in China, it may have applicability to other developing countries in the Asia-Pacific (e.g. Vietnam). School leaders may wish to consult the typology, as well as the imperatives for approaching the design of curricula for host country national teachers' professional learning, as a guide.

Finally, it is hoped that this book will help to establish a future agenda for academics based in China. The main struggle for Chinese/China-based academics is how to write about China from the inside while not becoming so detached that it becomes parochial, incomprehensible, and irrelevant to an outsider. For 'outsider-within' (Adeagbo, 2021) academics such as myself (i.e. non-Chinese, but with experience of living and working in China and Chinese internationalised schools), the issue becomes how to move beyond an analysis of China that 'renders the country a flat caricature merely serving to reflect the ambitions and insecurities of those analysing it' (Franceschini & Loubere, 2022, p. 5). These struggles may be overcome through greater collaboration between Chinese and non-Chinese scholars, as well as methodological innovations, such as co-joining macro- and micro-level foci by considering, for example, the impact of recent regulation of the international school sector on teachers' ongoing motivation.

As to my own future academic journey, I plan to develop the typology by collecting data from more host country national teachers. Not only would this nuance the exiting categories of Returners, Reachers, and Remainers, but it would also likely identify new categories of teacher. I also plan to continue exploring host country national teachers' perceptions of the nature and purpose of international schooling and see whether these perceptions show evidence of the impact of recent reform on teachers' thinking and practice.

The end of every journey is the beginning of a new one. I hope this book inspires many new journeys.

References

Adeagbo, M. J. (2021). An "outsider within": Considering positionality and reflexivity in research on HIV-positive adolescent mothers in South Africa. *Qualitative Research, 21*(2), 181–194.

Akkerman, S. F., & Meijer, P. C. (2011). A dialogical approach to conceptualizing teacher identity. *Teaching and Teacher Education, 27*(2), 308–319.

Bailey, L. (2015). Reskilled and "running ahead": Teachers in an international school talk about their work. *Journal of Research in International Education, 14*(1), 3–15.

Bailey, L. (2021). International school teachers: Precarity during the COVID-19 pandemic. *Journal of Global Mobility: The Home of Expatriate Management Research, 9*(1), 31–43.

Bailey, L., & Cooker, L. (2019). Exploring teacher identity in international schools: Key concepts for research. *Journal of Research in International Education, 18*(2), 125–141.

Ball, S. J., & Nikita, D. P. (2014). The global middle class and school choice: A cosmopolitan sociology. *Zeitschrift für Erziehungswissenschaft, 17*(3), 81–93.

Bassey, M. (2001). A solution to the problem of generalisation in educational research: Fuzzy prediction. *Oxford Review of Education, 27*(1), 5–22.

BISE. (2023). *PGCE-China*. www.bise.org/pgce-china

Bright, D. (2022). Understanding why Western expatriate teachers choose to work in non-traditional international schools in Vietnam. *Teachers and Teaching, 28*(5), 633–647.

Bukhari, S. G. A. S., Jamali, S. G., Larik, A. R., & Chang, M. S. (2023). Fostering intrinsic motivation among teachers: Importance of work environment and individual differences. *International Journal of School & Educational Psychology, 11*(1), 1–19.

Bunnell, T. (2016). Teachers in international schools: A global educational "precariat"? *Globalisation, Societies and Education, 14*(4), 543–559.

Bunnell, T., & Poole, A. (2022). (Re) Considering "precarious privilege" within international schooling: Expatriate teachers' perceptions in China of being marginalised and undervalued. *Educational Studies*, 1–15.

Cambridge Assessment International Education. (2023). Cambridge professional development qualifications. *Cambridge Assessment International Education*. www.cambridgeinternational.org/support-and-training-for-schools/professional-development/professional-development-qualifications/

Cambridge English. (2023). English teaching qualifications. *Cambridge English*. www.cambridgeenglish.org/teaching-english/teaching-qualifications/

Clandinin, D. J. (2016). *Engaging in narrative inquiry*. Taylor & Francis.

Cutri, J. E. (2022). *The localisation of Australian elite education within China: A case-study of various social actors' experiences at a Sino-Australian senior school* [Doctoral thesis, Monash University]. https://doi.org/10.26180/21323604.v1

Dos Santos, L. M. (2019). Recruitment and retention of international school teachers in remote archipelagic countries: The Fiji experience. *Education Sciences, 9*(2), 132.

Franceschini, I., & Loubere, N. (2022). *Global China as method*. Cambridge University Press.

Garton, B. (2000). Recruitment of teachers for international education. In M. Hayden & J. J. Thompson (Eds.), *International schools and international education: Improving teaching, management and quality* (pp. 145–157). Kogan.

Gaskell, R. (2019). The growing popularity of international K-12 schools in China. *ICF Monitor*. https://monitor.icef.com/2019/04/growing-popularity-of-international-k-12-schools-in-china/growing-popularity-of-international-k-12-schools-in-china-2/

Hagage Baikovich, H., & Yemini, M. (2022). Parental engagement in international schools in Cyprus: A Bourdieusian analysis. *Educational Review*, 1–18.

Hammer, L. L. (2021). *Exploring the ethnic gap in teacher salaries in international schools* [Doctoral thesis, Wilkes University]. Proquest. www.proquest.com/openview/870eda82d9e626ed0bd31833924eaa53/1?pq-origsite=gscholar&cbl=18750&diss=y

Hardman, J. (2001). Improving recruitment and retention of quality overseas teacher. In S. Blandford & M. Shaw (Eds.), *Managing international schools* (pp. 123–135). Routledge Falmer.

Hayden, M., & Thompson, J. (2013). International schools: Antecedents, current issues and metaphors for the future. In R. Pearce (Ed.), *International education and schools: Moving beyond the first 40 years* (pp. 3–24). Bloomsbury Academic.

Hrycak, J. (2015). Home and away: An inquiry into home-based and overseas teacher perceptions regarding international schools. *Journal of Research in International Education, 14*(1), 29–43.

IBO. (2023). IB educator and leadership certificates (IBEC). *IBO*. www.ibo.org/professional-development/professional-certificates/

Khalil, L., & Kelly, A. (2020). The practice of choice-making: Applying Bourdieu to the field of international schooling. *Journal of Research in International Education, 19*(2), 137–154.

Lee, M., Mo, Y., Wright, E., Lin, W., Kim, J. W., Bellibas, M., Faigen, B., Gumus, S., Ryoo, J. H., & Tarc, P. (2022). *Decoding the IB teacher professional: A comparative study of Australia, Canada, China, Denmark, South Korea, Taiwan, Turkey, and the United States*. International Baccalaureate Organization.

Lin, E., Shi, Q., Wang, J., Zhang, S., & Hui, L. (2012). Initial motivations for teaching: Comparison between pre-service teachers in the United States and China. *Asia-Pacific Journal of Teacher Education, 40*(3), 227–248. http://doi.org/10.1080/1359866X.2012.700047

Ma, Y., & Wright, E. (2021). Outsourced concerted cultivation: International schooling and educational consulting in China. *International Studies in Sociology of Education*, 1–23.

Maxwell, C., & Yemini, M. (2019). Modalities of cosmopolitanism and mobility: Parental education strategies of global, immigrant and local middle-class Israelis. *Discourse:*

Studies in the Cultural Politics of Education, 40(5), 616–632. https://doi.org/10.1080/01596306.2019.1570613

Namraksa, S., & Kraiwanit, T. (2023). Parental expectations for international schools in the digital age. Universal Journal of Educational Research, 2(1), 1–7.

Pollard, C. L. (2015). What is the right to do: Use of a relational ethic framework to guide clinical decision-making. International Journal of Caring Sciences, 8(2), 362–368.

Poole, A. (2016). "Complex teaching realities" and "deep rooted cultural traditions": Barriers to the implementation and internalisation of formative assessment in China. Cogent Education, 3(1), 1156242.

Poole, A. (2017). Interpreting and implementing the IB learner profile in an internationalised school in China: A shift of focus from the "profile as text" to the "lived profile". Journal of Research in International Education, 16(3), 248–264.

Poole, A. (2019). International education teachers' experiences as an educational precariat in China. Journal of Research in International Education, 18(1), 60–76.

Poole, A. (2020). Constructing international school teacher identity from lived experience: A fresh conceptual framework. Journal of Research in International Education, 19(2), 155–171.

Poole, A. (2021). International teachers' lived experiences: Examining internationalised schooling in Shanghai. Springer Nature.

Poole, A. (2022a). Beyond the tyranny of the typology: Moving from labelling to negotiating international school teachers' identities. Educational Review, 74(6), 1157–1171.

Poole, A. (2022b). Examining "precarious privilege" in international schooling: White male teachers negotiating contract non-renewal. Educational Review. Advance online publication. https://doi.org/10.1080/00131911.2022.2106190

Poole, A. (2023). A tale of two performativities: When performative learning meets performative technologies in a private language school in China. Journal of Education for Teaching. Advance online publication. www.tandfonline.com/doi/abs/10.1080/02607476.2023.2191838

Poole, A., & Bunnell, T. (2023). Teachers in "international schools" as an emerging field of inquiry: A literature review of themes and theoretical developments. Compare: A Journal of Comparative and International Education. Advance online publication. https://doi.org/10.1080/03057925.2023.2212110

Poole, A., & Li, X. (2023). Beyond a one-size-fits-all approach: Considering English language teachers' differential capacities for engaging in and implementing professional learning in China. Professional Development in Education. Advance online publication. www.tandfonline.com/doi/abs/10.1080/19415257.2023.2189284

Poole, A., Liujinya, Y., & Yue, S. (2022). "We're away from everything": Understanding the struggles faced by internationalized schools in non-urban contexts in China. Sage Open, 12(1), 21582440221081026.

Quinn, C. (2019). The country where over 260k ESL teachers work illegally. The Pie News. https://thepienews.com/analysis/china-esl-teachers-work-illegally/

Rey, J., Bolay, M., & Gez, Y. N. (2020). Precarious privilege: Personal debt, lifestyle aspirations and mobility among international school teachers. Globalisation, Societies and Education, 18(4), 361–373.

Savva, M. (2013). International schools as gateways to the intercultural development of North-American teachers. *Journal of Research in International Education, 12*(3), 214–227.

Schewel, K. (2020). Understanding immobility: Moving beyond the mobility bias in migration studies. *International Migration Review, 54*(2), 328–355.

Soong, H., & Stahl, G. (2021). Negotiating "global middle-class" teacher professionalism: Using transnational habitus to explore the experiences of teacher expatriates in Shanghai. *International Journal of Qualitative Studies in Education*, 1–14.

Su, Z., Hawkins, J. N., Huang, T., & Zhao, Z. (2001). Choice and commitment: A comparison of teacher candidates' profiles and perspectives in China and the United States. *International Review of Education, 47*(6), 611–635. http://doi.org/10.1023/A:1013184026015

Tarc, P., Mishra Tarc, A., & Wu, X. (2019). Anglo-Western international school teachers as global middle class: Portraits of three families. *Discourse: Studies in the Cultural Politics of Education, 40*(5), 666–681.

Van Oord, L. (2007). To westernize the nations? An analysis of the International Baccalaureate's philosophy of education. *Cambridge Journal of Education, 37*(3), 375–390.

Wright, E., Ma, Y., & Auld, E. (2022). Experiments in being global: The cosmopolitan nationalism of international schooling in China. *Globalisation, Societies and Education, 20*(2), 236–249.

Wu, W., & Koh, A. (2022). Being "international" differently: A comparative study of transnational approaches to international schooling in China. *Educational Review, 74*(1), 57–75.

Yang, L., Xie, Y., Zhou, A., Zhang, W., & Smith, J. (2023). The impact of the implementation of "double reduction" policy on tutors in shadow education: Legislation goals and early experiences. *Compare: A Journal of Comparative and International Education*, 1–17.

Ye, W., Ding, Y., Han, X., & Ye, W. (2022). Pre-service teachers' teaching motivation and perceptions of teacher morality in China. *Educational Studies*, 1–18.

Yemini, M., & Maxwell, C. (2018). De-coupling or remaining closely coupled to "home": Educational strategies around identity-making and advantage of Israeli global middle-class families in London. *British Journal of Sociology of Education, 39*(7), 1030–1044. https://doi.org/10.1080/01425692.2018.1454299

Yemini, M., Maxwell, C., Wright, E., Engel, L., & Lee, M. (2023). Cosmopolitan nationalism as an analytical lens: Four articulations in education policy. *Policy Futures in Education*, 14782103231168672.

Young, N. A. (2018). Departing from the beaten path: International schools in China as a response to discrimination and academic failure in the Chinese educational system. *Comparative Education, 54*(2), 159–180.

Index

accidental teachers 10, 85
American style (meishi) schools 25–26
Australian style schools 26–27

Bailey and Cooker (2019) 9–10, 84–85
Bian zhi 55–56
British style (yingshi) schools 26

China as method approach 11–14, 35
Chinese Dream 49–50
Chinese internationalised schools 27–29, 32
Cosmopolitan nationalism 28, 93

development of the international school sector in China 29–33
double reduction policy 61, 69, 91

ethics of typologising 86–87

Guoji rencai 13, 46–47, 49, 50

Haigui 13, 47–48
Hukou 59, 64

immobility 65–67, 69
international capital 47, 51
international school regulation in China 33–37, 71, 89

international school teacher motivation 7–9, 78–81
international school teacher typologies 9–11, 82–83

pedagogical capital 91–92
positionality 14–15
professional qualification for host country national teachers 88–89, 90–94

reachers 55–65
remainers 65–73
returners 46–55
Rey, Bolay and Gez (2019) 10, 84

Schools for Children of Foreign Personnel 22–23
Sino-Canadian style (zhongjia) schools 26
spatial continuity 66, 69

teacher motivation 6–7
teaching profession in China 56–57
typology of host country national teachers 82–83

Wai di 59

Xiaokang parents 13, 67–68

For Product Safety Concerns and Information please contact our EU
representative GPSR@taylorandfrancis.com
Taylor & Francis Verlag GmbH, Kaufingerstraße 24, 80331 München, Germany

www.ingramcontent.com/pod-product-compliance
Lightning Source LLC
Chambersburg PA
CBHW071512150426
43191CB00009B/1503